Guidelines for Christian Parents

by Walter H. Werner
Harold F. Tuggy
Theodore H. Epp
Mrs. Theodore H. Epp
and Robert S. Peterson

A
BACK TO THE BIBLE
PUBLICATION

Back to the Bible

Lincoln, Nebraska 68501

115,000 printed to date—1978
(5-7304—5M—38)
ISBN 0-8474-0723-3

Printed in the United States of America

Foreword

We are repeatedly asked questions related to leading children to Christ and helping them grow in Christian truth and principles. In past years we have had various authors write on different phases of this all-important area of responsibility. Their materials, with the exception of "Family Devotions," have appeared as articles in the *Good News Broadcaster*, the adult Bible study magazine published by the Back to the Bible Broadcast.

Since new homes are constantly being established and older homes are still asking for help, we decided to make this material available in book form. Thus this constructive information will have a continuing ministry.

A little overlapping is inevitable in a series of this nature, but that is good, since several authors write from the background of their own experiences.

This book should be helpful not only to parents but also for Christian workers who deal with children through ministries such as Bible clubs, Bible camps and Sunday schools.

—The Publishers

Contents

Family Devotions
by Robert S. Peterson

How to Lead a Child to Christ

by Walter H. Werner

Walter H. Werner has had wide experience in dealing with children. He was a pastor for a number of years before he joined the ministry of the Child Evangelism Fellowship. He served as that organization's director for Kansas, later for a 5-state region and finally for a 12-state region. He is no mere theorist but writes from a rich background of knowledge and experience. This material was first printed in the January and February, 1967, issues of the *Good News Broadcaster*.

How to Lead a Child to Christ

Have you noticed how much the Lord loves children? While He loves all mankind with a pure, infinite love, His heart seems to have an especially tender spot for children.

Perhaps this is because they are helpless, tenderhearted and open to both good and evil. He seems to love them just as they are—lambs having the Shepherd's greatest concern and needing His greatest care.

The Lord Jesus Christ showed this special love to them in wanting them near Him, in rebuking those who interfered, in demanding that adults become like little children in order to enter the kingdom of God and in setting a little believer up as the greatest in the kingdom. He even uses the title "children of God" instead of "adults of God" to refer to those who trust Him as their Saviour. How He loves the children!

God's method for propagating the human race is of exceeding interest. In love He draws two of the opposite sex together, and by His wisdom and power reproduces their kind. But even more interesting and marvelous than this is His propagation of the heavenly race. How does He do this?

In love the Holy Spirit works through a believer to draw a sinner and the Saviour together. The result is a newborn babe in Christ. You may be the believer. The Lord may begin the wonderful work simply by planting a desire in your heart to see a particular child saved. If so, consider how He will use you in doing it.

Preparation

God's first work is preparation. He will draw the child to Himself by you—a prepared, living vessel. He will instruct you, show you difficulties and how to overcome them and prepare your heart. Then you must follow the Holy Spirit and rely completely on Him.

The Spirit will lead you to see that by nature the child turns away from God, not toward Him. In Isaiah 53:6 we read: "All we like sheep have gone astray; we have turned every one to his own

8

way." And Romans 3:10 declares: "There is none righteous, no, not one." He will show you that the child needs to be completely turned around. This requires a new nature, which can result only from new birth in Christ. Matthew 18:11 makes this clear: "For the Son of man is come to save that which was lost."

The Lord uses only a small but absolutely essential part of the Bible to bring the child from spiritual death to spiritual life; it is the gospel. Romans 1:16 states: "For I am not ashamed of the gospel of Christ: for it is the power of God unto salvation to every one that believeth." The content of this power of God is given in a nutshell in I Corinthians 15:1,3,4: "I declare unto you the gospel. . . . That Christ died for our sins according to the scriptures; and that he was buried, and that he rose again the third day according to the scriptures."

The Lord can also instruct you by revealing His method of working in winning the child. He always draws individuals to Himself; He never drives them. In tender love Jesus said in John 6:44: "No man can come to me, except the Father which hath sent me draw him." And He said in John 12:32: "And I, if I be lifted up from the earth, will draw all men unto me."

Do you really want to lead children to Christ? The Lord will use you if you want to do it out of love for Him and love for lost children. He will show you how to overcome every difficulty. A heart of love overcomes fear. First John 4:18 says, "There is no fear in love; but perfect love casteth out fear: because fear hath torment." Just ask the Holy Spirit to fill your heart with love, and trust

Him to do it. Galatians 5:22 states that "the fruit of the Spirit is love."

Hindrances

In seeking to lead children to Christ, you will need to anticipate hindering factors and circumstances. There will often be opposition and disturbances. The Christian's enemies—the world, the flesh and Satan—are always a menace. But all of these should only challenge your faith in the Lord. He is more than able to overcome them all and will do it if you ask Him and trust Him to do it. As He does it, be sure to thank Him.

Perhaps the greatest difficulty to overcome is self. We naturally have a strong tendency to think we know something or can do something of ourselves. It is easy to forget that Jesus said in John 15:5, "Without me ye can do nothing." This tendency toward independence may be overcome by praying about it frequently, asking the Holy Spirit to keep us aware of our total helplessness and His ability to do all the work in and through us. It does not matter how many children we may lead to the Lord. It is most important that we always depend completely on the Lord to do the work. Philippians 2:13 explains, "For it is God which worketh in you both to will and to do of his good pleasure."

Before you lead a child to Christ, your heart, as well as the child's, must be prepared. Ask the Lord to completely control you, and believe that He is doing it. Then ask Him to prepare the child's heart so that he will be ready to accept the gospel and the Saviour. The Holy Spirit will not fail you.

10

Presentation

Having committed everything to the Holy Spirit, your one duty is to follow Him. He will direct your thoughts and actions. Follow Him in joyous expectation and watch Him work. He will bring you to the right child, alone or in a group. Always deal with the child as an individual—salvation is personal.

Imagine now that you are with a child or a group of children. The work of bringing the child and the Saviour together has begun. Your looks, attitude and actions should express love toward the child. Love—the love of Jesus—in your heart is the language every child understands. As a mother loves her baby, let the Saviour love the child through you.

Five Simple Steps

In bringing the lost child to Christ, the Holy Spirit will lead you to use simple verses in the Bible and very simple words. His work may be seen in these five simple steps—revealing God's love to the child, convicting the child of sin, presenting the Saviour, leading the child to receive Christ, and giving the child assurance and a sense of security.

With older children a verse of Scripture may be used for each step—I John 4:19 for step one, Romans 3:23 for step two, Romans 5:8 for step three, John 1:12 for step four and I John 5:12 for step five. But for younger children the use of just one verse for all five steps is usually wiser. John 3:16 contains God's great plan of salvation and falls into five simple divisions: (1) "For God so

11

loved" (2) "the world," (3) "that he gave his only begotten Son," (4) "that whosoever believeth in him" (5) "should not perish, but have everlasting life."

In demonstrating this to the child, the five fingers of the left hand may be used. The thumb stands for God, who loves; the index finger is the world, or the sinner, who is loved by God; the middle finger is the Son, the Saviour who died on the cross; the ring finger is the sinner who receives Christ; the little finger is the believer, who has eternal life.

View the situation from God's angle: He *attracts* the child, He *accuses* the child of guilt, He *acquaints* the child with the Saviour, He *acquits* the child of sin and finally He *acquires* and *assures* the child of salvation.

In using John 3:16 to deal with the child, you may present these five steps:

God loves you and wants you to belong to Him.

Do you know that God loves you? This is what the Bible says in John 3:16: "For God so loved the world, that he gave his only begotten Son, that whosoever believeth in him should not perish, but have everlasting life."

Do you know who God is? The Bible tells us that He is the One who made this world and everything in it. He made the animals, the birds, the fish and all the trees and flowers. He made everything for us because He loves us. He made all the people too.

God wants you to belong to Him so that He can take care of you. He is always good to you.

12

Because He loves you, He wants to give you every-thing that is good for you. God knows all about you. He sees you all the time. He knows what you are thinking. He knows all you do. He hears all you say. You cannot hide anything from Him. He loves you.

You can't belong to God the way you are because you are a sinner.

Do you know what sin is? Sin is anything that goes against what God has said. To steal a pencil or a piece of candy or some money is sin. To say a naughty word is sin. If you don't do what your mommy and daddy tell you, it is sin. And to hit or to hurt somebody is sin too. A sinner is a person who thinks, says or does wrong things.

Why do we think, say and do wrong things? Because we have a sinful nature—we were born that way. Something in us wants to do wrong things. This means that we have sin in our hearts.

What does sin do? The Bible tells us that sin comes between us and God. Because we have sin in our hearts, we don't love God and we can't hear His voice. We are afraid of Him, and we try to hide from Him.

But God still loves us, even though we sin. Our verse, John 3:16, says, "For God so loved the world." The "world" means the "people." You are one of the people, and you are a sinner. God loves you and wants you to belong to Him, but you can't belong to Him while you have sin in your heart. Your sin must be taken away.

Our verse says that God loved the world and that He gave His only begotten Son. He gave Jesus to us to take away all of our sins.

Jesus died for you. That's why God gave Jesus to us. Jesus was nailed to a cross to die for our sins—for your sins. He had no sins of His own, but God put all our sins on Him while He hung on the cross. We should have been nailed to the cross for our sins, but Jesus took our place. He took your place.

While Jesus hung on the cross, His blood ran out of His wounds for our sins. And He hung there until He died. That is the way God the Father gave His Son to us to take away our sins. The Father did it because He loves us. And Jesus willingly died for us because He loves us too.

After Jesus died on the cross, two of His friends took His body down. They wrapped it in clean, white linen and buried it in a tomb. This tomb was a hole in a big rock. Then they rolled a big stone in front of the tomb. He was buried, and all of our sins were buried with Him. All of His friends were sad.

But Jesus didn't stay dead; after three days He rose from the dead. He showed Himself to His friends, and they were very glad. At first, some of them wouldn't believe that He was alive again. But when He showed them His wounds, they believed and rejoiced. Then He went up to heaven again. He is alive now and will never die again.

14

Just open your heart and let Jesus come in.

Do you believe that Jesus died for you? The Bible says He did. It says that Jesus paid for all of your sins—not with money but with His precious blood. You can't take away your own sins. Only Jesus can do that. Do you want Him to take away your sins? Then you need to open your heart and invite Him to come in.

Will you invite Him to come and take away your sin now? All you need to do is to say to Him something like this: "Dear Jesus, I know I am a sinner. I believe that You died for me. Come into my heart and take away my sins." Our verse says, "For God so loved the world [you], that he gave his only begotten Son [to die on the cross], that whosoever [that means you] believeth in him [that means to open your heart and ask Him to come in] should not perish [remain dead spiritually], but have everlasting [eternal] life." Just close your eyes and bow your head and ask Him to come in.

Jesus gives you everlasting life.

Did you ask Him to come into your heart? What did He do in your heart? To whom do you belong now? Did He give you everlasting life? That's the kind of life you need in this world, and it is the kind of life you must have to go to heaven.

Let's read the verse again: "For God so loved the world [that's you], that he gave his only begotten Son [to die on the cross for you], that whosoever [that's you] believeth in him [that means to invite Him into your heart] should not

15

perish [not be lost forever], but have everlasting life."

Did Jesus give you everlasting life when you invited Him into your heart? He did! How do you know? Because I say so? No, because the Bible says so.

What would you like to say to the Lord Jesus since He loved you, died for you and took away your sins? Would you like to thank Him? Just bow your head and thank Him out loud. He is listening.

Because you can believe what the Bible says about the Lord Jesus Christ, you can believe it when it says that you belong to Him. He loves you and will take care of you. So you must listen to Him and do what He wants you to do.

Dealing With Children in a Group

Children in a group tend to follow a leader. To avoid this, ask them to close their eyes while you request a show of hands as a response to the invitation. Those who respond in this way should be dealt with individually and thoroughly. Ask questions and give the child an opportunity to explain what took place.

When it is clear that a child has simply followed a leader without understanding what salvation is all about, he should be dealt with in love and patience. The five steps should be clearly and slowly presented again. If the Holy Spirit is drawing the child to the Saviour, he will be saved. If not, you need to wait for the Spirit to enable the child to understand the truth. A person cannot be coerced into believing.

16

Do not conclude that the child is saved because he raised his hand. A desire to be saved should not be mistaken for the new birth. If the decision—which must be made—is of the Lord, it will show itself by expressed conviction of sin and should lead to regeneration. The desire to be saved involves a necessary longing to be free from sin, while the new birth results in a new creation and demonstrates itself in a new life that did not exist before.

This new life shows itself in the fruit of the Spirit—love, joy and peace. It also shows itself in new desires. There will be a desire for the Lord, for prayer, for the Bible and for fellowship with God's people. The child should also desire to tell others about Jesus so that they may be saved too. If the child shows no evidence of the new life, the explanation of salvation must be repeated.

Do not expect a child's conviction of sin to be as strong as an adult's. Children have not been as involved in sin as most adults have. But there must be conviction, or they will have no desire to be saved. Salvation is from sin and its consequences. Conviction results in a sense of guilt. Evidence of this guilt may take such noticeable forms as sadness, confession, tears or fear. Where there is no indication of conviction, more time needs to be spent in explaining God's hatred for sin, its consequences and His deep desire to forgive that sin. Emphasizing the crucifixion and its meaning often brings the needed conviction.

17

Another difficulty is the danger that a child may exercise a natural faith instead of a spiritual faith. All children are born with a natural faith. Children readily believe almost everything they hear. This characteristic carries over into every experience, including the area of salvation. But when it comes to receiving Christ as Saviour, this natural faith is entirely worthless and means nothing. For salvation, another kind of faith is required. This faith is a direct gift of God and comes to the child through the Holy Spirit as the gospel is given. Without this gift of a spiritual faith the unsaved child cannot receive Christ and eternal life in Him.

Ephesians 2:8 refers to this valid, living, working faith: "For by grace are ye saved through faith; and that not of yourselves: it is the gift of God." And Romans 10:17 says: "So then faith cometh by hearing, and hearing by the word of God." What the child says and does will help you to discern whether the faith is natural or spiritual.

False Security

One more difficulty which you may encounter is a sense of false security on the part of the child. This often happens when a child has been allowed or led to believe that salvation has taken place when it has not. This is a serious mistake and can lead to serious consequences. Regeneration must take place or the child certainly is not saved.

Such a false security may be detected by asking the child, "How did you become a Christian?" If

18

the child's reliance is on anything but Christ and the Word of God, it is a false assurance. God's Word makes it clear that Christ does both the saving and the keeping. True faith relies on Christ for both the work of the new birth and that of godly living. This gives the security that cannot be shaken.

If you have just led a child to Christ, it is time to rejoice. All heaven is rejoicing (Luke 15:7), so why shouldn't you, the "spiritual parent" of the child? God's redeeming love has won, and it will never cease.

Like the physical birth of a child, the work of winning a child to Christ has three distinct phases—preparation, presentation and promotion. The first two have already been considered. The third phase—promotion—involves getting the newborn babe in Christ off to a good start in godly living.

Promotion

Although regeneration is the greatest thing that can happen to an individual, it is but the beginning of all the wonderful living and growing that follows. Who should take the first steps in helping the new arrival in the family of God? Wouldn't this logically be the responsibility of the one who brought the child to Christ?

How can this be done? First, always allow God's great love to fill your heart and flow through you to this new Christian in every way possible. God's love in you will make this responsibility a great privilege and joy, not a duty. Love cannot forget or forsake its object.

Because of your deep love for the child you will want to give some clear, simple instructions about daily prayer, Bible reading and doing God's will. The latter should include instruction concerning confession of sin (I John 1:9) and witnessing to others (Ps. 107:2). Also get the child's full name, along with the parents' names, address and phone number. Learn something about the child's home life, the father's or mother's occupation and church affiliation, if any.

Give the child a tract to take home to read and follow. It should clearly explain at least three things—what took place at salvation, what it means to be a Christian and some guidelines about what a Christian should or should not do.

By your own daily prayers you can help both in securing the Lord's protection of the child against sin and in promoting godly living. The child will experience victory or defeat largely according to your specific prayer or lack of it. James 5:16 says, "The effectual fervent prayer of a righteous man availeth much." Do you want to accomplish great things in the life of the child? Then learn how to pray effectively, and do it daily. We sin against other Christians by failing to pray for them (I Sam. 12:23).

You may also promote the growth of the new Christian by several personal contacts in the first few weeks after the new life has begun. When this is not possible, you will want to see that the child is placed under the spiritual care of another competent Christian. This could be the parents of the child, a godly relative or friend, a Sunday school teacher or other children's worker or a pastor. Be sure to make this arrangement yourself.

You can further promote the young believer's spiritual growth by introducing him to a sound, Bible-believing, Bible-teaching church. Such a church has a place waiting for the child who has just been saved. Here the child will enjoy Christian fellowship, receive the necessary continuous instruction and learn to participate in the life, worship and work of a body of believers. Every child needs a godly home and a spiritual church home. A godly home and a spiritual church work together as a team to equip the child with God's best for this life and for eternity.

It will not be easy in every instance to find a good church and once found, to successfully get the child involved in that church, but every effort should be made to do it. In addition, the child will be greatly helped if he is encouraged to attend a sound children's Bible class during the week.

Building a Christian Home

by Harold F. Tuggy

Harold F. Tuggy is a veteran missionary serving under the Orinoco River Mission in Venezuela. This material was first printed in the April—June, 1965, issues of the *Good News Broadcaster*. Christian parents found the subject matter very biblical, informative and practical.

The Four Walls of a Christian Home

"Except the Lord build the house, they labour in vain that build it" (Ps. 127:1).

Just as four walls are the minimum essential in the building of a house, so are four disciplines essential in the Christian home. As the walls enclose the house, making it a unit and protecting the inhabitants, these four disciplines hold the home together and protect the family from many deadly temptations.

Christian parents must practice these disciplines in their own lives and prayerfully and diligently seek to build them into the lives of their children. They will not build in vain if they build

22

these four walls around their homes, for they are biblical principles.

Reverence

Reverence is the first wall. "Thou shalt not take the name of the Lord thy God in vain" (Ex. 20:7). "Keep thy foot when thou goest to the house of God. . . . For God is in heaven, and thou upon earth: therefore let thy words be few" (Eccles. 5:1,2). "But the Lord is in his holy temple: let all the earth keep silence before him. . . . O Lord, I have heard thy speech, and was afraid" (Hab. 2:20; 3:2).

A child should learn reverence at home. When Father opens the Bible, all should listen reverently to the reading; it is the voice of God speaking. Then all should kneel in His presence and present their petitions. Even the smallest child can sense God's presence and be silent.

Once I pinched my brother and laughed with him during family prayertime. Father sent me to my bedroom, and when the time of devotions was finished, he came in. I saw tears in his eyes, which made me understand how deeply he was hurt by my lack of reverence. He explained to me how serious my offense was, and then he punished me—which took all the fun out of pinching my brother during devotions.

Respect for Parents and Elders

The second wall—respect for parents and elders—joins the first wall to form a corner. As two

23

walls are mutually strengthened by the union at the corner, so these two disciplines are dependent on each other, and each strengthens the other. Where one is lacking, the other will be lacking also. The child who does not obey his parents will not have reverence for God.

"There is a generation that curseth their father, and doth not bless their mother. There is a generation that are pure in their own eyes, and yet is not washed from their filthiness. There is a generation, O how lofty are their eyes! and their eyelids are lifted up. There is a generation, whose teeth are as swords, and their jaw teeth as knives" (Prov. 30:11-14).

"Honour thy father and thy mother" (Ex. 20:12) is the first commandment given with a promise. In the law of Moses, the persistent infraction of this commandment carried a death penalty.

This is another lesson that my father taught us. He was not a harsh man but was a quiet and gentle man who was also firm and just. When he said something, we children understood that he meant it. And if he told us to do something, he may have had to tell us a second time, but it was best not to make it necessary for him to speak a third time! And no one ever dared to say, "No, I'm not going to do that."

When my wife and I were newlyweds, we lived in a little house next to another Christian family. A double garage served both houses. The other family had no children of their own but had an adopted boy. One day the mother and the boy were out in the garage. The mother asked him to help her. He talked back to her and flatly refused. I had learned from my parents that you just do not talk that way!

In the years we have been teaching in Las Delicias Bible Institute in Venezuela, we have seen many students come and go. It does not take long to discover which ones have not learned to respect their parents. They are spoiled, ill-mannered, saucy, proud and insolent. If during their first or second year in the institute this defect is not overcome by the grace of God, we recognize that they will not become effective Christian workers. Regardless of how much consecration they may profess to have, they will not be effective.

Truthfulness

Truthfulness is the third wall. "Lie not one to another, seeing that ye have put off the old man with his deeds" (Col. 3:9).

This is a clear command that we are not to lie. Lying is of the old nature, and it is an innate characteristic of the human heart. A child does not have to be taught to lie. The new birth in Christ and death to the old nature is the only remedy.

But even Christians are sometimes deceitful, and deceit is sin. When a home lacks this wall of truthfulness, it often lacks the walls of reverence to God and obedience to parents also. Falsehoods and hypocrisy undermine the foundation. Truthfulness involves honesty to others and to oneself. The Word of God is the judge of honesty in motives, plans and actions. This integrity is the protection and confidence of the Christian home.

The parents must be scrupulously honest before they will be able to teach their children honesty. Honesty must be built into the children's characters in the home.

Purity

The fourth wall is purity. "Mortify therefore your members which are upon the earth; fornication, uncleanness, inordinate affection. . . . But now ye also put off . . . filthy communication out of your mouth" (Col. 3:5,8).

Moral filthiness is also a part of our old nature, and it is everywhere around us. Many publications and television programs glorify lust and are full of immoral implications. This is also true of certain kinds of music heard on radio and television. These things have no place in a Christian home. Carefully evaluate what your children see and hear. Don't take anything for granted.

Because the world is corrupt and Satan is clever, many dangers surround our families. With God's help, build solidly and well these four walls—reverence, respect for parents and elders, truthfulness and purity—to protect the moral and spiritual welfare of your home.

Principles of Child Discipline

Those who are first learning to drive an automobile often have a tendency to oversteer. The car moves toward the left side of the road, and the learner reacts by turning the wheel to the right, but he turns it too far. Then as the car heads for the right curb, the amateur driver gets scared and pulls the wheel to the left, but again he turns it too far.

Many parents are like beginning drivers in disciplining their children. They are alternately too soft and too severe. As a result the child becomes confused, discouraged and sometimes even enraged because he has no consistent standard to go by.

The Apostle Paul admonished us twice in his writings not to provoke our children to wrath (Eph. 6:4; Col. 3:21). This indicates that he had observed an abuse of parental discipline. Nothing will anger or discourage a child more than unfair and inconsistent discipline.

Discipline has two aspects—the negative and the positive. Negative discipline says no. It makes prohibitions and prescribes and executes punishments. Positive discipline directs the activities of the child in a constructive and educational way. It requires an intelligent study of the character, interests, abilities and needs of each child and is, therefore, more difficult.

Many parents overuse negative discipline and make little or no effort to use positive discipline. Both are as necessary as the positive and negative poles of a magnet.

The following paragraphs discuss some guidelines concerning the negative aspect of discipline.

Parents Must Be Agreed

Agreement between parents is a prime requirement for good discipline in the home. If there is a difference of opinion between the father and the mother, they need to work it out privately and come to an agreement. They must present a united front to the children. "United we stand, divided we

27

fall" is perhaps more true in the home than any-where else.

Bobby asks his mother if he can go out and play ball. Mother says, "No, you haven't cleaned up your room yet today." Then Bobby runs to his father as he comes home from work and asks, "Daddy, can I go out and play with the boys?" Daddy tells him he can. Later, Mother sees Bobby out playing and calls, "Bobby, you come here this minute! What are you doing out there? Didn't I—"

"But Daddy said I could."

We parents have all been tricked into this sort of situation. Children soon learn to play one parent against the other.

Who was in the wrong? Obviously, Bobby was. But both parents were also wrong. Why? This was probably not the first time that Bobby had played one against the other—not if he is big enough to play ball with the boys. He had done it many times before and had got away with it.

The parents should explain to Bobby that when one parent makes a decision, he is not to run to the other parent to get his way before the parents have had an opportunity to discuss the matter. Bobby is big enough to understand this. If Bobby continues to play one parent against the other, he should receive appropriate punishment.

Sometimes a third party in the home, such as a grandparent, will interfere in the discipline of a child. The grandparent should know better, but if he does not, it becomes the very unpleasant duty of the parents to tell the grandparent kindly and respectfully—but firmly—to keep out of such affairs.

28

In child training, "let your yea be yea; and your nay, nay" (James 5:12). Both parents must always agree.

Attack Lying—Never Deceive Your Children

Jeremiah 17:9 says that "the heart is deceitful above all things, and desperately wicked." Deceitfulness is a part of the old nature that we inherited. It shows itself in children amazingly soon after birth. As previously stated, a child does not have to learn to lie; it is part of his nature.

Lying not only involves words spoken with the purpose of deceiving but also any action that is designed to deceive. Some parents allow their children to deceive them—they shut their eyes to little indications of underhandedness. Soon the child becomes an expert at the art of deception. Every evasive answer or excuse should be followed as a detective would follow a clue until the full truth is discovered.

One Christmas my two brothers and I received a little red wagon. At the time, we were eight, six and four years old. A new house was being built two blocks from where we lived. One day we picked up a few bricks and brought them home in our little red wagon. The few bricks that some little boys could carry in their wagon were of insignificant value to the contractor. But when Dad came home from work and saw the bricks, he saw something more—he saw the moral value that was very significant.

"Arthur! Harold! Paul! Where did you get those bricks?"

"We found them."

"Where did you find them? Was it down there where they are building that house?"

Suddenly we found something very interesting to look at on the floor, but we had to confess the truth. We were told to take the bricks back.

"But the men might see us taking them back!"
We were hoping that Dad would forget, but the next day when he came home from work, he said, "Harold, have you taken those bricks back?"

"N-no. I-I forgot." (I might have invented a more original excuse.)

We knew then that Dad was not going to forget. So three small boys, like three puppies with their tails between their legs, unloaded some bricks from their little red wagon behind a brick pile on the corner. We have never forgotten that lesson.

But many parents would have accepted the first evasive answer, "We found them." It would be much less trouble, but it would do the children a great disservice. Lying must be attacked decisively.

How can we teach our children truthfulness if we lie? Did you ever send your child to answer the doorbell and tell him to say that his mother was not at home? Or have you ever told your child that you were going over to the neighbors for a few minutes and that you would be right back, when in reality you were going shopping? If so, do not be surprised when he comes up with an evasive answer, a weak excuse or a bold lie. Whatever you sow you will also reap (Gal. 6:7).

Punishment in Proportion to the Offense

Some parents would spank a child severely for breaking a dish but would laugh to hear them use a swear word. To break a dish has no moral implications other than a minor act of carelessness and usually not even that—it is most often merely an accident. A patient word of caution and instruction should be sufficient. But obscene speech has serious implications and should be dealt with immediately.

Chastise Decisively

Threats, nagging and little slaps do no good. If the offense is worthy of punishment, make it a punishment that the child will remember and will not want to receive again for a similar offense.

Our daughter once grabbed her older brother by the neck and began choking him to force him to give her something she wanted. Her mother gave her a hard spanking which our daughter never forgot. "How cruel," some would say. But it would have been much more cruel to have allowed her to continue that little trick. One day in a fit of anger she might have choked her brother to death. This offense demanded decisive punishment, and she got it. She never attempted to choke her brother again.

Did this provoke her to wrath? No! She understood very well the justice of the punishment. A child does not resent fair punishment.

Do Not Punish When You Are Angry

The child understands whether his parents punish him out of anger or whether they discipline him justly for corrective reasons. If it is merely to vent the parent's anger, then in Paul's language, it provokes the child to wrath (Eph. 6:4). When the parent is angry, the chastisement is likely to be much more severe than it should be. Therefore, if you are angry, wait until your anger has passed; then explain to the child the reason for the punishment, and then discipline him calmly and deliberately. At the same time, remember that discipline should be administered within a reasonable time after the incident of wrongdoing or the child may not fully realize why he is being punished.

Use a Variety of Correctives

Spanking does not correct some children. One little boy was promised a whipping if he did a certain thing. His answer was, "Then I'll laugh." And he did. But if he was denied his dessert or was kept in the house when the other boys were out playing, this was effective punishment.

My younger brother, Paul, went through the "playing-with-fire" stage. He would steal matches from the kitchen and build his little fires in the yard with paper, sticks and dry grass. Our parents spanked him repeatedly but to no avail. One day Mother found him building his fire very close to the house.

Finally Dad bought a dozen boxes of matches—the kind that had wooden sticks about 2½ inches long. Then he fixed a shield so that the wind would not spread the fire and sat Paul down to the fun of burning matches. At first it was lots of fun—but before long it became a task. Dad went off to work and left Mother in charge.

Before long we heard, "Mama, I've lit enough matches."

"Oh no, Paul, you just keep on lighting matches."

Soon Mother found him striking three, four or five matches at a time.

"No, Paul, you must burn them one at a time, and let them burn clear down to the end."

By nine o'clock Paul was watching the matches burn through his tears. Mama phoned Dad to see if she could stop the match-burning. (Note that both parents were together on this.) Father said Paul was to keep on. By ten o'clock the tears were putting out the fire. Another telephone call was made, and Dad ordered the burning stopped. Never again did Paul steal matches from the kitchen.

All parents need is a bit of originality and imagination to keep ahead of the children.

Correct Your Mistakes

Since parents are human, they sometimes make mistakes. When you find that you have done the wrong thing—made an arbitrary decision, punished the wrong child or lost your temper—go to the child you have wronged and make it right. This is only fair. We should not think that because we are adults we have a right to violate our children's sense of justice and fairness. On the contrary, because they are in their formative years and their feelings are delicate and tender, we must take great care not to hurt them. By admitting it when we are wrong we will keep their confidence and respect.

33

If you promise a child a spanking, spank him. If you promise him an ice cream cone, give him an ice cream cone.

"Now, Jimmy, if you do that again, I'm going to spank you!" Jimmy does it again.

"All right, Jimmy, I told you I was going to spank you if you did that again. OK, now you know. If you do it again, I'm going to beat you within an inch of your life."

Jimmy's mother has already lost the battle. Jimmy knows that he will not be punished the third time or the tenth time! His mother made many threats but did not follow through with any action. The mother's mistake is in not keeping her word and spanking Jimmy the first time he repeated his offense.

"Now, Johnny, you stay home with your sister and Ginny, and when we come home we'll bring you some candy." So Johnny's parents drove off to the nearby city to go shopping.

When Johnny heard the car turn the corner a couple of hours later, he ran to the door calling, "Here comes Mama with my candy—my candy!"

When his mother saw Johnny and heard his excited and happy expression, she said, "Oh, Honey, we forgot about Johnny's candy. Don't stop the car; let's go on around the corner to the grocery store and buy Johnny's candy." It was unthinkable to disappoint Johnny. To him, the candy represented his parents' word of honor.

John was three then. Now he is grown and married and has a little girl of his own. But he still has a deep respect and love for his parents because of that candy and the principle of fairness and honesty which his parents followed throughout the years.

Every child needs direction, correction and instruction, and above all he needs to have the security of a confidence in something bigger than himself. Parents who exercise firm, fair and loving discipline inspire this kind of confidence. By keeping their word and by establishing and requiring the observance of sound rules in the home, parents can provide the stability and source of confidence which is a fundamental need of the mind of the child.

"Children, obey your parents in all things: for this is well pleasing unto the Lord" (Col. 3:20).

"He that spareth his rod hateth his son: but he that loveth him chasteneth him betimes" (Prov. 13:24).

If the rod of correction is applied according to these rules, it will be for the good of the child. With the Holy Spirit's guidance and working in our lives and the lives of our children, we will rear children who will please God—and us—not only at the present time but also in the years to come.

Guidelines for Rearing Children

A father had been careless about the discipline and the moral and religious instruction of his son. When the son grew up, he became a criminal and was a fugitive from the law for a long time. The father, now old, lived alone. Late one night the son came and took his father out into the woods.

There he showed him an old tree that was twisted and ugly. He ordered his father to straighten the tree and threatened to kill him if he did not. The father answered in surprise, "Son, how can you demand such a thing? If the tree were young and the wood soft I could tie a pole beside it so that it would grow straight. But now it is impossible."

"I am that tree," answered the son. "When I was a child you should have corrected and instructed me. Now I am old and hardened. It's too late."

The Scriptures command parents to bring up their children "in the nurture and admonition of the Lord" (Eph. 6:4). This verse commands positive discipline. It speaks of rearing our children, of intelligently directing their development and of guiding their activities. It speaks of teaching them under divine direction and with instruction correctly related to God and to His Son Jesus Christ. Parents are obligated to lead their children in the way of the wisdom which has its beginning in the fear of the Lord.

Positive and instructive discipline requires thought and preparation. The parents must carefully observe the character and development of each child. Children are individuals, each differing from the other; therefore, it is necessary to guide each one individually.

We must thoughtfully pray and strive to train our children so that they will become wholesome Christian citizens. The following principles will help in this difficult task.

Parents must live Christian lives that are consistent with their profession. A father cannot teach his children to be gentle and humble if he himself has fits of anger. He cannot teach them purity of thought and speech if, even in unguarded moments, he uses vulgar language. A mother cannot teach her daughter to be truthful if she sends her to the door to say that Mother is not at home.

Some children of Christian parents are not following in the way of the Lord. Why? In many of these homes there is some serious inconsistency in the life of one or both of the parents. Perhaps the father and mother quarrel or the father orders his children harshly and despotically or the mother has an uncontrolled tongue. The parents should live such exemplary Christian lives that they can say with Paul, "Be imitators of me, just as I also am of Christ" (I Cor. 11:1, NASB).

Family devotions should be geared so that the smallest child can understand and participate. Sing a children's hymn or a chorus. Read a Scripture portion that is easy for children to understand. Explain it to them in simple words. Make the prayer short and simple. Teach each child to pray in words that he will understand. The prayers of children are sweet music in God's ears.

Above all else, work and pray until each child is truly born again. Do not take their spiritual life for granted. Do not believe the cliché which says that your children are "little angels on leave from heaven." If you do, you will soon smell smoke on their wings! Do not believe that a child is born

37

again simply because he sings hymns or says a memory verse in Sunday school.

A child does not have to be very old to understand. One year, a few days before Christmas, Esther looked up at her father and said, "Daddy, you know what I am going to give Jesus for Christmas? I am going to give Him my heart." And she did. We never had reason to doubt the sincerity of her commitment, even though she was not five until the following March.

One of our boys was a clever little fabricator and deceiver until he gave his heart to the Lord. After that we never again had reason to doubt his word. If the old tendency had continued, we would have doubted the sincerity of his conversion, for God's Word says, "No lie is of the truth" (I John 2:21).

Job got up early in the morning to make sacrifices and to pray for his children because, as he said, "It may be that my sons have sinned, and cursed God in their hearts" (Job 1:5). Do as Job did. Pray for your children and do not rest until you are sure that they are all true Christians.

Guide the Activities of the Family

It is important that the family do things together. Eat together, read together, play together, work together. This provides opportunity for the parents to guide the children's activities.

A thoughtful effort is required to keep conversation at the table wholesome and instructive. There are always interesting articles and books to be discussed. You may want to talk about football scores or baseball championships or what happened at school.

Some families use one meal each day for Scripture memory work—reviewing portions learned and learning new ones. Guessing games can be very instructive. In Twenty Questions one person thinks of some historical or biblical person. The rest of the group tries to find out who it is within the limit of 20 questions that can be answered yes or no. The person who guesses the right answer then gets to think of the next character. Some families use dictionary games. These games are based on words that are similar in meaning (synonyms), words that are pronounced alike but have different meanings (homonyms), rare words, or words whose true meaning is often misunderstood.

Read together. Few families ever sit down to read an interesting article or book together. Television has taken the place of reading, causing a great cultural loss.

Work together. A family can share many projects around the house. Together they can enjoy one another's company and accomplish necessary duties.

Play together. Many families enjoy swimming or biking or skating or camping together, and they build the family into a solid unit as they enjoy these activities with one another.

Give Your Children Something Constructive and Educational to Do

It is not enough to tell a child not to do this or that. He must be given something constructive to

39

do to replace the undesirable activity. His mind is active, and his body is full of energy. If a child is not given a worthwhile project, the Devil will give him something to do. He has plenty of work for idle hands.

Children four or five years old can learn to sew. How proud little girls are of their "beautiful" doll dress! Mother, take a minute to admire that dress, and then tactfully show your child how to improve her work.

With some parental guidance and help, a child of six or eight can build a simple birdhouse or put together and paint a box for storing "treasures"—stamps, rocks, grains or whatever. Children can learn to safely use garden and shop tools at a reasonably early age; as a result, they will be more useful to themselves and to others as they grow up.

While we were visiting in a home, the 12-year-old boy of the family took us to his room. With pride he showed us his aquarium. He had fish, tadpoles, turtles and other kinds of aquatic life which he was studying. Someday that boy may be a marine biologist. But what would have been the result if his mother had said, "No! No! Get them out of here! You can't have those slimy things in the house"? A child who is discouraged by his parents will look for companionship elsewhere—often in places where he should not go.

Some children like tadpoles and frogs; others like tools. Some like to sew; others like to draw and paint. The important thing is that the parents encourage and direct their children in profitable activities such as these.

A three-year-old can learn to hang up his clothes. A child of six can learn to clean his room, and when he is ten, he can be responsible for washing the supper dishes or preparing breakfast. The important thing is to assign duties to each child according to his age and abilities and to firmly insist that these tasks be done. If we assign a task but do not demand its fulfillment, we have done nothing but teach irresponsibility.

"Peter, please take out the trash." An hour later his mother finds Peter out playing ball with the trash still sitting there. She should not tell John, who is not doing anything, to do Peter's job. She should call Peter in and demand that he do his task. Then he can go out and play. It may be necessary to repeat this lesson with firmness many times, but Peter will finally learn that he must work first, then play. If Peter gets away with shirking his duty, the battle is lost, and Peter will never learn responsibility.

There are some disagreeable jobs that must be done. These should be given to the children by turns and without partiality. These jobs have to be done whether we like them or not, and a child must learn this lesson.

Cultivate the Companionship and Confidence of Your Children

I was sitting at a table fixing an alarm clock. Our oldest boy, then three, shoved his head up between my arm and the table. "Daddy, I want to

41

see." Should I have told him to get away because he would break something or to run along because I was busy? This would have hurt his feelings and would have alienated him from me. His confidence in me was worth more than any old clock. I put him on a chair where he could watch but not touch. Now he is a man, and he knows how to repair anything from a fine Swiss watch to a diesel engine. Best of all, he has always been close to his father.

"Mom, I want to help you wash the dishes."
"No! You get out of here; you'll break something. You always want to get in the way."

The child goes away crying, her little heart broken. The mother keeps talking to herself: "That kid always wants to stick her nose in where she shouldn't." The mother does not understand that she has lost a wonderful opportunity to cultivate the companionship and confidence of her daughter as well as to teach her something. When the girl reaches adolescence and needs the confidence and counsel that only her mother should give, she may seek the advice of friends and may receive perverted instruction.

A girl once said to me concerning a friend she knew intimately, "There is nothing that enters her mind that she would not feel free to tell her mother." Why did this girl of 18 have such confidence in her mother? From infancy her mother had cultivated her companionship. They worked together, read together and talked together, and the mother never wounded her tender heart.

It is better for the neighbor children to come and play in your yard than for your children to run all over the neighborhood to play. It will be more trouble for you to have your yard full of neighbor children, but you can know what your children are doing, what they are talking about and what kind of language they are using. They should be where they can be seen. As long as they are running, jumping and yelling, everything is probably all right. But when they are hidden and quiet, it is impossible to know what they may be doing or what they may be talking about.

You *must* know where your children are and what they are doing. You must not shut your eyes to reality—the world and the Devil have a thousand ways to corrupt the minds of your children.

Make the Home an Attractive Place
Where the Children Will Want to Be

A home that is lived in and has a hospitable and friendly atmosphere has far more attraction than one with luxurious furnishings that lacks these elements.

In the living room of my mother's home was a piano that had been bought only by sacrifice. All of us children had taken music lessons, and that had cost an additional sacrifice. One brother played the trumpet. We had many happy hours playing and singing together. During high school days our friends would come to our house to do their homework. At times my sister would make fudge. Mother, who was then a widow, was always

43

with us, a good companion and counselor but never nagging or scolding. Even friends who were not Christians enjoyed the friendly atmosphere. A Christian testimony was always maintained. Mother knew where her children were and what they were doing because she made our home attractive.

It takes thought, sacrifice, work and self-control to follow the guidelines mentioned in this chapter. But to do so will produce wholesome results. Bring your children up "in the nurture and admonition of the Lord" (Eph. 6:4).

Effective Child Training

by Theodore H. Epp

This series of studies by the founder and director of Back to the Bible was first given on the Broadcast's daily 30-minute program. It appeared later as a series of articles in the July-August—November, 1966, issues of the *Good News Broadcaster*.

A Christian's Responsibility to Children

One of the most important subjects of our day is effective child training. How they can properly fulfill this responsibility is the deep concern of most Christian parents. To these parents is given this remarkable promise from God: "Train up a child in the way he should go: and when he is old, he will not depart from it" (Prov. 22:6).

Not only does God encourage us, He also teaches us how to meet this grave responsibility of properly training our children. These instructions are found in both the Old and the New Testaments.

The Lord said to the Israelites in Deuteronomy 11:18-21: "Therefore shall ye lay up these my words in your heart and in your soul, and bind them for a sign upon your hand, that they may be as frontlets between your eyes. And ye shall teach them your children, speaking of them when thou sittest in thine house, and when thou walkest by the way, when thou liest down, and when thou risest up. And thou shalt write them upon the door posts of thine house, and upon thy gates: that your days may be multiplied, and the days of your children, in the land which the Lord sware unto your fathers to give them, as the days of heaven upon the earth."

Trained in the Word

The first basic principle that God gives in these verses is that children are to be trained in the Word. It is to be taught to them regularly and is to be consistently brought before them. In one of his letters to Timothy, Paul referred to his young disciple's early training. Paul wrote: "But continue thou in the things which thou hast learned and hast been assured of, knowing of whom thou hast learned them" (II Tim. 3:14). The apostle went on to state when it was that Timothy was first introduced to these matters: "And that from a child thou hast known the holy scriptures, which are able to make thee wise unto salvation through faith which is in Christ Jesus" (v. 15). Timothy's grandmother and mother were instrumental in instructing him in the Word from his early childhood, according to II Timothy 1:5. This basic

46

instruction resulted in salvation when Timothy was brought face to face with the gospel as an adult.

This has been true in the experience of many others, even some who became wayward, sinning against the spiritual light that had been given to them in their early years. Then, because of the grace and mercy of God, the Bible knowledge that had been implanted in them in their formative years finally resulted in the salvation of these individuals.

A Memorized Verse

Some time ago I read of a fatally wounded soldier who asked his general for spiritual help. The soldier said, "Sir, will you please tell me how to die? I am not ready."

The general made fun of him, saying, "Young man, I don't believe that nonsense in the Bible. You are all right. You have given your life for your country, so everything will be all right."

But the young man would not give up. He continued to plead for help.

Finally, the general, who had lived many years as an unbeliever, said to him, "If this helps you any, I just remembered a verse my mother taught me when I was a child. I don't believe it, but it says, 'God so loved the world, that he gave his only begotten Son, that whosoever believeth in him should not perish, but have everlasting life' " (John 3:16).

The wounded man had him repeat the verse until its meaning was clear. Then he died, having found peace in Christ.

Many years later, when the general was retired, he found that the memory of that verse would not leave him. He decided that since it had brought peace to a dying soldier, there must be something to it. So he himself accepted the Lord Jesus Christ as his personal Saviour.

In this case, a Bible verse was memorized by a boy who did not believe it. Yet, when it was repeated at the deathbed of a soldier, it brought that soldier to a saving knowledge of Christ. Later, the one who had memorized the verse as a child was saved in his old age through it. This demonstrates the grace of God, but it also demonstrates the power of the Word when memorized in childhood.

Are We Concerned?

God's concern for the spiritual well-being of children is sometimes reflected in the lives of His people. And this is as it should be. Many of us have felt responsible not only for our own children but also for the children of our neighbors who sometimes care nothing for Christianity. The Lord has called into being a number of good organizations that are reaching children for Christ; but regrettably, some Christians seem to have no burden for children other than their own.

Jonah had a similar attitude toward Nineveh and Israel. He was instructed by God to warn Nineveh of impending judgment if they did not change their ways. But instead of carrying the message, he fled in the direction of Tarshish. Jonah did not want that Gentile nation spared and said to the Lord: "I knew that thou art a gracious God, and merciful, slow to anger, and of great kindness,

48

and repentest thee of the evil" (Jonah 4:2). Without regard to what judgment would have meant to Nineveh, Jonah wanted to die rather than live when he saw that God had spared the city.

God had to teach Jonah a lesson. He raised up a gourd to protect the prophet from the heat of the sun. Then the Lord caused a worm to attack the gourd so that it withered. Jonah became angry at this, and God said to him: "Doest thou well to be angry for the gourd? And he said, I do well to be angry, even unto death" (4:9).

Jonah was completely dissatisfied with the way God was handling the situation at Nineveh. The prophet was self-centered and was concerned only for Israel's welfare. He cared nothing for that great Gentile city. His experience of three days and three nights inside the fish had made him willing to give the message of warning to Nineveh, but it did not change his true attitude. He was still unhappy to see God act in mercy and not in judgment.

He was like many today who are discontented with reaching others with the gospel, because the methods which some employ do not suit their church or their own ideas of what is best under certain circumstances. They would rather watch young people and children perish than to cooperate with organizations outside their own church circles.

Surveys show that a substantial number of young people leave the church during their junior-high years and that most who accept Christ as Saviour do so before the age of 18. This demonstrates the need for reaching children and young people with the gospel.

49

Jonah went east of Nineveh and made a booth so that he could sit in comfort and see what would happen to the city. Like Jonah, some of us are satisfied to sit in earthly comfort and watch a world go to hell. We see destruction approaching, but we never lift a finger to help lost sinners. We complain about juvenile delinquency, yet we do nothing to reach the juveniles. God's Word still says that we should train a child in the way he should go, and when he is old he will not depart from it (see Prov. 22:6).

The Lord, the Bible says, raised up the gourd to protect Jonah and to deliver him from his grief. And "Jonah was exceeding glad of the gourd" (Jonah 4:6).

Similarly, people today are often smug and satisfied in their prosperity. However, God has allowed us to prosper so that we can evangelize the world as well as our own children.

Just a generation ago more young people had surrendered to God for missionary work than the missionary societies could absorb. Today mission organizations are crying out for young people and are not finding enough of them. What is the reason? Our generation has not trained our children.

We have become too fascinated with our prosperity. We ignore the fact that God has given us prosperity in order to prepare us and a younger generation to send the gospel to the ends of the earth. God has provided us with a wide open door to reach the hearts of our own children, but soon that door will be closed.

To help make Jonah aware of his attitude, God sent a worm to attack the gourd and cause it to wither (4:7). In the same way, God may allow setbacks to arouse today's Christians to their responsibilities. He may even permit persecution to fall on His people.

Physical suffering is certainly indicated in the following verse in Jonah: "And it came to pass, when the sun did arise, that God prepared a vehement east wind; and the sun beat upon the head of Jonah, that he fainted, and wished in himself to die, and said, It is better for me to die than to live" (v. 8). Sometimes suffering or persecution may be necessary to awaken us to our responsibilities.

The leaders of Communist countries try to shield their children and youth from exposure to the Bible and its teachings. They feel that adults are beyond the reach of the gospel. Hitler emphasized youth and youth training, and it was that trained younger generation he used in accomplishing his goals.

God showed Jonah how inconsistent it was for him to have great concern for the gourd and yet to have no consideration for the people of Nineveh. One fact that God stressed was that in Nineveh there were 120,000 children who were unable to discern between their right and their left hands (v. 11). Jonah had forgotten this, but God had not. The saving of Nineveh was due in part to her children.

Is God sparing America today because of its children? This could be the reason, for the older generation appears to have little concern for the things of God.

Children delight the Lord; our Saviour used this fact in teaching a severe lesson to the disciples and to us. The Lord Jesus placed a child before His followers and said, "Except ye be converted, and become as little children, ye shall not enter into the kingdom of heaven" (Matt. 18:3). He went on to say, "Whoso shall receive one such little child in my name receiveth me. But whoso shall offend one of these little ones which believe in me, it were better for him that a millstone were hanged about his neck, and that he were drowned in the depth of the sea" (vv. 5,6). This is a most solemn statement, and we should be careful to heed it.

Train Up a Child

A key verse concerning the believer's responsibility for training children properly in the things of God, which was given previously, is Proverbs 22:6: "Train up a child in the way he should go: and when he is old, he will not depart from it."

This was the responsibility given to the people of Israel by God. Speaking through Moses, He said, "And ye shall teach them your children, speaking of them when thou sittest in thine house, and when thou walkest by the way, when thou liest down, and when thou risest up. And thou shalt write them upon the door posts of thine house, and upon thy gates: that your days may be multiplied, and the days of your children, in the land which the Lord sware unto your fathers to give them" (Deut. 11:19-21).

But why train a child? Why not wait and begin with an adult? The reason is not hard to see. The years of childhood are the formative and impressionable years.

Children find it easy to memorize scripture, but it is often difficult for adults.

Character and habits are formed in childhood and during the teen years. Studies show that most of a person's habits are formed before he reaches the age of 20. This is true for both good habits and bad. Nearly all alcoholics became entrenched in the drinking habit before they were 21 years of age.

Childhood is also the age of faith. During those years the beliefs that will govern the rest of a person's life are fixed. What a person believes after he is in college will depend to a great extent on what he was taught in his early, formative years. When a young person's Christian faith is destroyed in college, the reason is not altogether due to what the college teaches. What was implanted in the heart and mind of that student in his childhood is also important. If genuine faith has been implanted and nourished in a young person's heart, he can stand true to Christ even in the worst environments.

Moses was trained in his own home in his formative years. This training may not have extended beyond his 10th or 12th birthday, but it influenced him in the 30 years during which he was trained by the Egyptians. What he learned from them was not designed to cultivate his faith in God. Instead it included instruction in idolatry, with all its false values and untruth. Nevertheless, Moses stood true to what he had learned in his father's house.

53

One well-known branch of organized Christendom has been credited with saying, "Give me a child until he is seven, and I will have him the rest of his life."

Conscientious Christian parents have been seeking to meet the challenge of secularism in our day. There are an increasing number of Christian grade schools, Christian high schools and Christian colleges. More are needed. Not all Christian parents can send their children to such schools even where they are available. However, one poor excuse is often made for not sending children to such schools. Some parents say, "I will not send my child to a Christian school because I don't want to make a 'house-plant Christian' out of my child."

The one who originated that statement was the Devil himself. This was the very thing he suggested to Adam and Eve when he tempted them in the garden. He intimated that God was making house plants out of them by placing restrictions on them. They needed to reach out for themselves and do as they pleased—then their eyes would be opened. Then they would be like God and know what was good and what was evil.

We might as well tell the farmer that he should not cultivate his corn, because if he does, he will make house plants out of it. He ought to let the weeds grow so that the corn will have competition and learn how to stand on its own. Training a child in the way he should go is something like cultivating a crop. The weeds must be removed to insure the best possible harvest.

Three elements are involved in training a child—education, example and discipline.

By definition, education is transmitting to the child the knowledge and experiences of humanity. For example, we know by experience that electricity can be harmful and also beneficial. We transmit this knowledge to the child so that he will avoid the dangers and learn to apply the powers of electricity in useful ways.

The same is true in the spiritual realm—there is a correct path to follow and there are wrong paths to avoid. The child needs to know which way he should go. Children are imitators and want to do what they see their parents do. They also learn a great deal from one another, so parents should be careful about who their children's playmates are.

Children imitate. They develop habits by using other people for examples. They see these examples at home, at church and at school. Can secular schools give our children the Christian examples they need to follow? Children are pliable during the early years, and this is when they should be exposed to the best Christian examples.

Discipline is the third element needed in training a child. Some parents have very vague ideas about what discipline involves. They oversimplify. They think that if a child does something wrong, the only kind of discipline is spanking. Physical punishment is important, but discipline involves much more than that.

Discipline may be defined as a method of instruction in education that seeks to make the doing of right a pleasant task and the doing of wrong an

55

unpleasant task. This definition can be applied in many ways. When children do something wrong, we punish them in one way or another. This impresses on them the fact that doing wrong brings unpleasant consequences. But if this is all we do, we are failing. We also need to show them that doing right is pleasant and is followed by pleasant results.

If we are to train a child in the way he should go, we will have to bring him or her to Christ. Jesus said, "I am the way, the truth, and the life: no man cometh unto the Father, but by me" (John 14:6). This is a basic fact, but what are we doing about it? We send our children to school five days a week and they spend five to six hours a day there in preparation for this life. Then we send our children to Sunday school one day a week where they receive 30 to 45 minutes of biblical instruction. In many cases this is the only training they receive for eternal life. How mixed up can we get?

Not all parents have access to Christian schools for their children, but even Christian schools cannot take the place of home training. Proper training in the home is the basic essential if parents are to meet their responsibility.

Why a Decline?

Why is there a decline in the proper training of children today? The breakdown of the home is one reason. Many homes have no family devotions. How many take time each day to meet with their children and study the Bible? Time must be taken every day for Bible reading, singing and prayer. If we are so busy with other family, school and church activities that we have no time to train our children for God, then we are in trouble.

The industrial revolution is a second cause for the decline in the proper training of children. An industrial revolution as such is not morally or spiritually wrong. But it can cause serious problems when it disrupts home life because both parents are working and the preschool child is put in the care of a baby-sitter who knows nothing about Christian child training. This is a serious matter that many parents need to face.

Part of this problem stems from trying to live up to the high economic standards of present-day living. It consumes a great deal of a person's time to produce an income adequate for the kind of life he may want to live. Then many find that they have no time left to spend with their families.

What is the remedy for this? It involves setting priorities. Training a child calls for discipline in the lives of the parents too. But when they do what God commands, they can claim the promise that the child, when he has grown up, will not depart from his early training. This is God's promise, and He will see that it is carried out.

None of us chooses his heredity—the physical and psychological characteristics transmitted to us by our parents. We are born with certain abilities and tendencies. Heredity, however, can be adversely affected by improper training or improper environment. To train children to give in to their evil natures is to make them children of hell. On the other hand, if we train a generation of born-again children, we will stabilize the home, the church and the nation.

Christian parents have the power to mold the future church, the future society and the future nation. No man lives to himself, and no man dies to himself. And we are all affected by the things we see and hear. The program God designed for training children in the way they should go is the only answer to the moral and spiritual decline we see around us.

When to Begin Spiritual Training

How early should the spiritual training of a child begin?

The Apostle Paul wrote in his second letter to Timothy concerning Timothy's faith: "When I call to remembrance the unfeigned faith that is in thee, which dwelt first in thy grandmother Lois, and thy mother Eunice; and I am persuaded that in thee also" (II Tim. 1:5).

This passage, of course, tells us that Timothy was a third-generation believer. Both his mother and his grandmother had maintained a vital testimony for Christ. Timothy followed their example. But at what age was his spiritual training begun? "But continue thou in the things which thou hast learned and hast been assured of, knowing of whom thou has learned them; and that from a child thou hast known the holy scriptures, which are able to make thee wise unto salvation through faith which is in Christ Jesus" (3:14,15). "From a child" indicates that Timothy was quite young when he was first taught the Scriptures.

I read some time ago about a mother who said she began training her child to talk when it was only a month old. Of course, the little baby could not understand what she said, but the mother used correct English and not baby talk. As the child's interest increased in the things around it, the mother began to name different objects and explain what they were. She said that it was surprising how soon her child began to speak.

When parents and friends use baby talk, they should not expect the child to learn to speak correct English. He has to unlearn the baby talk before he can learn to speak properly.

This, of course, has to do with natural learning, but what about the things of the Spirit of God? The name "Jesus" can become precious to children who have been taught to honor and revere His name at a very early age. It should be one of the first words a child learns to speak. Children can learn at an early age about love and sin and the need of Jesus as their Saviour.

The Place of the Mother

The mother is the key person in this training. She holds and cradles the child and can begin teaching him at an early age. The child's thinking should be molded from the very beginning. The right words should be used and the right truths stated even before the little ones can understand them. They learn by hearing things over and over again. It is the parents' duty to be sure that they hear the right things and learn to repeat the right things.

In a family with several children, the youngest will often begin to talk at an earlier age than the others did. The reason is that the older children will talk to the baby just as soon as he begins to pay attention to them. The same is true in the spiritual life.

Our children began to attend church as soon as their mother was strong enough to take them. In those earlier years we did not have nurseries in which to leave the little ones, so baby went with Mother. When the child was old enough to sit, he or she sat with Mother. And there was discipline in the pew.

A small child can hardly be expected to sit quietly all the time, but the mother can take along things to interest the child that will not distract others. At the same time she should insist on good behavior.

We made it a rule with our children that if we had to take them out of church because of their behavior, they were disciplined when we got home. This needs to be done only once or twice as a rule. They soon learn that they are expected to behave themselves while in church.

We also need to teach our children that there is a certain degree of reverence included in church attendance. It is not uncommon to find children, either before or after church, running all over the place as if they were on a playground. The church is not a recreation hall, nor is it home.

Parents should read Bible stories to their children. The stories should be as simple and clear as possible. You will be surprised how much little children understand. At first they may not comprehend a great deal, but by telling and retelling these Bible stories their young minds are molded into biblical patterns of thought. We need to start teaching our children before they begin playing with the neighbors. The time to begin is before the child can even walk.

Memory work should also begin early. In fact, it can begin just as soon as the child starts to talk. At this stage, verses must be very brief—perhaps just two or three words at a time. But persist in teaching them to the children.

My wife used to spend a half hour in the evenings with our children, going over their Bible verses with them before they were tucked in for the night. I can still remember that when they had learned their first Bible verse, they came in and repeated it for me. They were delighted with their accomplishment.

Gospel songs also have a place in training children. They should have the opportunity to listen to gospel songs before they are exposed to worldly music. They will learn to recognize hymn and gospel song melodies. Some children will even be able to hum the tunes before they can talk.

As far as factual knowledge is concerned, children know nothing when they first come into this world. But by the time they are three years of age they have learned a lot. Certain facts have been impressed on their minds by that time. Certain attitudes are locked within them. What impressions of soul and life do Christian parents implant in their children by the time they are three years of age?

The Father's Responsibility

The mother, of course, is responsible for much of this training because she is usually with the

61

children more of the time. However, the father bears a great deal of responsibility also. The Bible tells us that the father is to train the child in the Word of God, but that begins when the child is a little older. That is the time when the great basic truths of the Scriptures must be taught, simply but clearly.

The father also has responsibility with regard to discipline. Too often the father is called on when the mother has reached a point of frustration and does not know what to do. Then the child is left with the impression that the father's place in the home is that of a disciplinarian only.

Fathers must be careful concerning this matter. The Bible says, "Ye fathers, provoke not your children to wrath: but bring them up in the nurture and admonition of the Lord" (Eph. 6:4). The father must be fair and kind in discipline.

Begin early to let the children know that they are part of the family. Be practical in their training. Do not be satisfied to merely talk about Jesus and the Bible, but apply the life of Jesus to them and show them how the Word of God fits everyday life. They will come to see that Christ is not only an example but that He is their very life and lives in them.

Impress on them the fact that what the Bible says is what Jesus is saying to them. All of us will eventually be judged by the Bible. Be patient with children, for sometimes they respond readily and other times they do not. Sometimes fruit is immediate, while at other times we must wait quite a while to see results.

Teach your children to believe the Word of God and have faith that God will work within them. Trust the promises of God whether you see results in the children at first or not. "Train up a child in the way he should go: and when he is old, he will not depart from it" (Prov. 22:6).

Childhood is a time of faith. Children believe what they are told. So train them in biblical truths and principles in those early days before they go to school.

To let the children do what they please is to follow the path of least resistance. They do not have to be trained to do the wrong things. It is true that corn, when planted, will grow by itself, but it grows better when it is cultivated. There is no need to cultivate weeds, for they will grow almost in spite of us.

The depraved nature which we inherit is like the law of gravity. It constantly pulls us down to lower moral and spiritual levels. By ourselves, we can do nothing about it. We need divine help to overcome it. If we want to overcome the law of gravity, we need power to do so. This is also true in the spiritual realm. To do wrong, all we must do is let go. If we want our children to walk in the broad way which leads to destruction, we do not have to do anything about it. That is the road they will naturally follow. But if we want our children to be trained for the Lord, then we must take a definite part in this training, and we must begin early.

Biblical Examples

The Bible contains several illustrations concerning this very subject. King David of Israel was a remarkable man in many ways, but he was not without his failures. A number of his children turned out to be corrupt, but others were good men.

Adonijah, the fourth son of David, was born in Hebron while David was fighting against Saul. David apparently had no time for his children in those years, and some of the women he married were heathen. No wonder the Scriptures say of Adonijah: "Then Adonijah the son of Haggith exalted himself, saying, I will be king: and he prepared him chariots and horsemen, and fifty men to run before him. And his father had not displeased him at any time in saying, Why hast thou done so?" (I Kings 1:5,6).

At no time in his life had David corrected this son of his. He had completely neglected Adonijah's training.

The same thing was true of Absalom. His mother was the daughter of a foreign king, and because of his training, he became an evil man.

Solomon, on the other hand, was born after David had committed his great sin and had been forgiven by the Lord. David's own spiritual life had mellowed, and he gave more time to his family. Nathan was Solomon's tutor. His mother, Bathsheba, though a partner in David's sin, apparently had a good influence on Solomon's life.

Undoubtedly, it was Joshua's early training and the influence of Moses' example and counsel that brought Israel's second great leader to the place where he could say, "As for me and my house, we will serve the Lord" (Josh. 24:15).

Moses was destined to spend many years in the court of Pharaoh. Yet Moses was so well trained in the early, formative years of his life that he decided to suffer affliction with the people of God rather than to enjoy the temporary pleasures of sin.

Samuel was also a godly man, partly because of his early training in the things of the Lord. His parents took him to serve in the house of God when he was quite young. Unfortunately, like Eli before him and David after him, Samuel neglected his own sons in their formative years. They grew up to be wicked men who brought disgrace to Samuel and to God.

We must mold our children in the way they should go. Then when they are old, they will not depart from the correct paths mapped out for them.

Claiming Your Family for Christ

The Apostle Paul and his missionary companion Silas had been thrown into jail for preaching the gospel. Acts 16 tells us that Paul and Silas were praying and singing at midnight. Suddenly there was a tremendous earthquake that jarred the prison doors open, making it possible for the prisoners to escape. The jailer responsible for the prisoners had fallen asleep, and when he woke up he thought surely the prisoners had escaped.

The jailer was about to take his own life when Paul called out to him: "Do thyself no harm: for we are all here" (v. 28). The jailer recognized that what had happened was of God, and he asked Paul and Silas, "What must I do to be saved?" (v. 30). The answer that Paul and Silas gave him is one of the most significant statements of the Bible:

"Believe on the Lord Jesus Christ, and thou shalt be saved, and thy house" (v. 31).

Here is God's great promise of salvation for an individual and his family. Hours of worry and anxiety could have been spared many a Christian father or mother if he or she had recognized this precious promise and appropriated it by faith. The salvation of a believer's family is a precious truth revealed in the Holy Scriptures.

Proverbs 11:21 says, "The seed of the righteous shall be delivered." Delivered from what? Delivered from hell; delivered from the grip of the Devil; delivered from all that is opposed to our blessed Lord and Saviour. This promise is all inclusive. God, in His grace, has presented the believer with a check, to be drawn on God's own account, and the believer may fill it in according to the need.

What About Personal Faith?

Does the individual himself need to exercise faith to be saved? Yes, definitely. Ephesians 2:8 says, "For by grace are ye saved through faith." But you may ask, "If Paul said that the jailer's faith would bring salvation to his family and household, how does that correspond with the fact that each individual himself must have faith to be saved?"

The answer lies in the fact that the same faith which made it possible for the individual to be saved from condemnation will also bring his family to the place where they will personally trust Christ for salvation.

But suppose they do not believe? Then that could be the fault of the believer's lack of faith, for God has indicated that when one believes on the Lord Jesus Christ, his family will eventually be saved.

Have you accepted the first part of the promise—"Believe on the Lord Jesus Christ, and thou shalt be saved"? You cannot claim the second part—"and thy house"—until you have claimed the first part. If you have claimed the first part but do not believe the second part of Paul's statement to the jailer, then you lack faith to accept all that God's Word says.

If you believe in Christ as your Saviour, you will be saved. And, according to Paul's statement to the jailer, if you believe in Christ as your Saviour, your family will eventually turn to Christ for salvation. Just as surely as you have eternal life, you can be sure that your family will be brought to the same realization.

This, of course, includes the fact that one's family must be exposed to the gospel so God can bring everlasting salvation to them as a result of the believer's faith. That the gospel is to be given to the family for them to trust Christ is evident from Acts 16:32, which says that Paul and Silas spoke the Word of the Lord to all who were in the jailer's house.

The Bible says, "The mercy of the Lord is from everlasting to everlasting upon them that fear him, and his righteousness unto children's children" (Ps. 103:17).

The fact that a parent looks to God for the soul of his child does not keep the matter of salvation from being a personal act of faith, and by no means does it pave the way for an easy-going Christian experience. It ensures the dealings of God with your child on behalf of your faith, for salvation is of the Lord.

This is not saying that there is some kind of a covenant relationship, as is taught by some groups. Some think that when a child is born in a Christian home, he is in a covenant relationship in God's family, and the parents go through a ceremony to indicate this. I do not believe that this is taught by the Scriptures, and this is not what I am emphasizing. I am emphasizing only that when a person receives Christ as Saviour, he can, by faith, claim the salvation of his entire family for God. As the individual has faith in God concerning this matter, and the family is exposed to the gospel, they will eventually trust Jesus Christ as personal Saviour.

Noah and His Family

God told Noah, "Come thou and all thy house into the ark; for thee have I seen righteous before me in this generation" (Gen. 7:1).

Dr. Harry Ironside says about this passage: "It is the desire of God to save the household of His people. Noah's family found a place in the ark because of their father's acceptance of God, yet on their part there had to be obedience to the divine call. Invited by God, they entered the place of safety and so were saved, through the water, from the judgment that overwhelmed the world of the ungodly."

While Noah believed God for the salvation of his whole household, he made preparation for all of them. In response to Noah's faith, God was able to procure obedience through faith on the part of the family, and they, too, entered the ark.

Rahab and Her Family

When Joshua sent spies into Jericho, they were protected by Rahab (Josh. 2). Before the spies left, Rahab asked them to spare her and her household when the Israelites came to take the city. The promise was made that she and her household would be spared, which was done precisely as promised, for she believed and they then also believed and gathered with her in the place prescribed by the spies (2:12-21; 6:25).

Abraham and World Blessing

Abraham's faith is possibly the most outstanding illustration of individual faith that brought blessing to both a blood-related family and also to a spiritually related family. Abraham was called out from his country and home to follow the Lord. Genesis 12:1 tells of Abraham's call, and verses 2 and 3 record the promise of blessing God gave to him.

Because of this one man's faith, blessing has come on the whole human family. Each member of Abraham's family had to be brought to individual saving faith, but because of Abraham's faith, unconditional promises were made that included the whole world as recipients of the blessings of God. This incident involving Abraham's life reveals that God is able to benefit future generations by the faith of a single individual. Because of Abraham's faith, believers today enjoy the blessings of the gospel of the grace of God.

Joshua and His Family

An incident from the closing days of Joshua's life serves as an outstanding example of how one man, by faith, is able to claim something for his family. In his final challenge to Israel, after he had enumerated the wonderful blessings of God, Joshua said, "Choose you this day whom ye will serve; . . . as for me and my house, we will serve the Lord" (Josh. 24:15).

Joshua spoke firmly in behalf of his whole family. Did he speak prematurely? Between the time of his making the statement and the death of his family could not some in his family fail to trust God for salvation?

Joshua did not place his confidence in his own children but in the promise of God; he believed that God would honor his faith and bring each member of his family to salvation. Of course, Joshua would have been faithful in exposing his family to the truth of God so each member could make a personal response of faith.

David and His Family

The promise that God made to David included more than salvation; nevertheless, it is a promise based on God's promise of household blessing. God had previously promised Abraham that He would establish an everlasting covenant with him. Then

70

David, believing God, received the promise from God that his throne should be established forever (II Sam. 7:13). That promise is yet to be fulfilled at the return of the Lord Jesus Christ, who will sit on the throne of David.

There was also a New Testament illustration of God's principle of working with the family. It involved Cornelius, who believed that not only he himself would be saved but also his whole household. The result of the faith of Cornelius is clearly stated in Acts 10.

Faith Versus Worry

Many a mother who has prayed for the salvation of her children worries as she sees them go astray. Her prayer is not a prayer of faith based on the promise of God. It may be that she is ignorant of the promise of God that her faith will save not only herself but also bring her family to saving faith. Worry and faith do not go together. Where there is faith, there is no worry; where there is worry, there is no faith.

A promise which has helped many people is found in Philippians 4:6,7: "Be careful [anxious] for nothing; but in every thing by prayer and supplication with thanksgiving let your requests be made known unto God. And the peace of God, which passeth all understanding, shall keep your hearts and minds through Christ Jesus." If prayer is accompanied by faith, there can definitely be thanksgiving. True faith will bring such peace to a believer's heart that he can cease from worrying and give thanks to God for the accomplishment of faith right there and then.

71

As we consider family salvation, it does not necessarily mean that the family will come to know Jesus Christ as Saviour before the death of the parents. Such was the case with John. He was a straying child, but when his mother died, she had claimed salvation for all of her children. She said her faith was based on God's promise that salvation would extend not only to her but also to her household. Five years after her death, John rose in a meeting to say he had been brought to the Lord in answer to the prayers of his mother.

First Corinthians 7:14 says, "For the unbelieving husband is sanctified by the wife, and the unbelieving wife is sanctified by the husband: else were your children unclean; but now are they holy."

In this verse, the words translated "sanctified" and "holy" are derived from the same root word meaning "set apart." The unbelieving partner is not saved by living in the same house with a believing partner. However, he is set apart in an atmosphere where he can see the Word of God being lived out daily by his believing partner. So also, the children of Christian parents—or even of one Christian parent—are not Christians just because their parents are. But the children are set apart in such a family, for they are under the direct influence of the gospel. In such a setting, the Holy Spirit can use the Word and the prayers of the parent or parents to bring the children to see the need of trusting Jesus Christ as Saviour.

Take courage. You may be the only one of your family who is saved, but God's promise holds true. You may not see the results in your lifetime, but you can rejoice, by faith, in the salvation of your household. Pray, trust God, and He will bring it to pass.

Helpful Hints for the Christian Family

by Mr. and Mrs. Theodore H. Epp

Mr. and Mrs. Epp tell how they handled the problems faced by Christian parents in raising children in the nurture and admonition of the Lord. This chapter is adapted from material that first appeared in the March—December, 1963, issues of the *Good News Broadcaster*.

Helpful Hints for the Christian Family

"So God created man in his own image;... male and female created he them. And God blessed them, and God said unto them, Be fruitful, and multiply, and replenish the earth, and subdue it" (Gen. 1:27,28). "And Adam called his wife's name Eve; because she was the mother of all living" (3:20).

Parenthood is a blessing, but it also involves tremendous responsibilities. The first command that God gave to man was to be fruitful and multiply; therefore, it is well that we consider some of the varied aspects of parenthood—its blessings, responsibilities, joys and sacrifices.

74

The fact that man was created in the image of God and made especially for the glory of God implies that parenthood means much more than bringing children into the world. God also entrusts each of our children to us for proper upbringing and training. We are to prepare each child for the particular purpose for which God allowed him to come into the world. Thus, in a sense, we stand in God's place and are held responsible by God to give each child proper instruction and direction.

The first parents of the race had no parents. God brought them into the world fully mature and ready for the task He had for them. But as our first parents they became responsible to God for each of their children, and this has been God's program ever since.

Parental Preparation

You must begin praying for your child and preparing for his training long before he is born. Prospective parents should be preparing themselves for this new responsibility by dedicating themselves to the Lord, who alone is sufficient for such a far-reaching and awesome privilege.

Many instructions are given in the Word for fathers and mothers, especially in the Book of Proverbs. Character studies of Bible men and women provide helpful insights into the problems of family life. The epistles also contain much practical instruction along this line.

A father and mother must count the cost. Parenthood demands sacrifice. Anything worthwhile costs, but being a good father or mother demands an unusual amount of unselfishness and sacrifice. Many pleasures and ambitions must be put aside. Considering these matters before your child is born and preparing yourselves for the event will be a great step toward becoming good parents.

We, as parents, must always remember that God has entrusted us with a life that will continue throughout eternity. He entrusts us with the basic Christian training and upbringing of each child for Him so that His sovereign purpose will be worked out in that life. Each child actually belongs to Him, but we are given the privilege and responsibility of raising that child for His use.

A little child is to be led. We as parents are responsible for where and how his life is led and directed. As each new life comes into our home we can give the child back to God and, as Hannah said of Samuel, say, "For this child I prayed; and the Lord hath given me my petition which I asked of him: therefore also I have lent him to the Lord; as long as he liveth he shall be lent to the Lord" (I Sam. 1:27,28).

As we continually consider our children to be the Lord's, we should reverently wait on God for instruction and help from His Word. Prayer for the child should help instill in our hearts the joy and the responsibility of training him not only for his own good and ours but, above all else, for the honor of the Lord.

When to Begin Spiritual Training

Looking at that tiny baby who is so innocent and helpless draws from us as parents a love that causes us to protect and provide for the child. The

76

physical care of children is important, but we are not as likely to neglect that as we are their spiritual needs. In their spiritual development, however, we are not only to teach them but to train them.

For instance, how soon should the child be taken to church? The answer is obvious—as soon as the mother herself can go. The first place our children went was to church. We began to impress on them that they must be quiet in church. If this is done early, children will not be a problem there.

We personally cannot remember the first time we went to church. Church attendance was normal to our way of life and was the natural thing for us to do.

Long before a child can carry a tune, he is receptive to music. Mothers usually sing to their children, so why not sing gospel songs to them? It is surprising how easy it is to memorize such songs as they are sung over and over again. This will prove to be a great blessing to the mother and will add to the child's character as his ways of thought and action are being formed.

Sometimes, a child will even learn to sing before he or she learns to speak. And songs learned well in childhood are seldom forgotten. They are usually present as a tool for the Holy Spirit to use in the years ahead.

A Mother's Devotional Life

A mother with preschool children who has dedicated herself to a life of continual devotion to the Lord will have the problem of finding time and opportunity to be alone with God. No definite solution can be given for this problem. Mothers frequently find that when they try getting up before the children do, the children wake up earlier too. Sometimes the only really quiet time in the household is in the evening when the mother is often too tired to think clearly.

However, after carefully scrutinizing your family schedule with its problems and responsibilities, you may find some time for a short Scripture reading before the family gets up. Or you may find time to meditate on some thought and to commit yourself to the Lord for the day. But even these few minutes may be interrupted by some unusual situation. When this happens the mother should not feel guilty. We must remember that our faith should not be in our quiet time but in the Lord who reigns. Even in ministering to our family, our hearts can be, and must be, in communion with God. The Lord meets us in our circumstances.

During the time when the children take their naps, the mother may be able to arrange for a longer time of Bible study and intercessory prayer. This will necessitate putting other important tasks aside, which will not be easy. But the strength one receives from feeding on the Word is worth it. A mother can also use the time spent to feed an infant as a time of meditation and prayer. Having a Bible verse written on a card that she can have before her when doing her household tasks gives her an opportunity to meditate on and memorize a portion of scripture.

Many live in areas now reached by an increasing number of Christian radio stations. These outlets provide wholesome music and messages from

God's Word which can encourage and instruct a mother even while she is working around the home. Some programs are designed specifically for women, while others, such as the Back to the Bible Broadcast, are produced with the whole family in mind. The potential effect on children exposed to the day-long influence of Christian radio makes it all the more worthwhile to consider this supplement to the suggestions already made.

The Mother at Home

Since the early preschool years of a child's life are the most formative, a mother should be at home with her children during that time. A little child is content to play near the mother as she works around the house. A child wants to belong and finds a sense of security in being in the presence of his parents. The mother has little time that she can call her own, but these are years when she is molding lives. She is building character, giving her greatest contribution to mankind and doing her greatest work for the Lord.

The early years, when you can mold your children's lives, are few and pass very quickly, so use every waking moment. As a Christian mother you must begin early to tell them about God, creation, the love of God and God sending the Lord Jesus to us. Let these truths be their earliest recollections. Telling or reading Bible stories is very important. Truth is more easily understood and grasped by small children than fiction. The mother must acquaint herself thoroughly with the story so that she will not teach error. Emphasize that the

79

Bible stories are true. Storytelling can entertain your child as you work.

After hearing a Bible story, a child often begins to ask questions, so the mother has opportunities to enlighten the child's heart as he grows. This is true of all his questions, not just his spiritual ones. Thank God for a child who keeps you busy answering questions. When you are exhausted from answering questions, remember that you are building a life for the Lord. If you cannot answer a question, tell him that you do not know the answer. God has not revealed some things to us. Give no occasion for the child to doubt God. Let him know that we cannot always understand and explain God but that we believe what He says in His Word.

Get a good Bible storybook, and always close the day by reading at least one story to the children. These stories can be read consecutively until the entire Bible is covered and can be read over and over again. The children love to hear them repeated. We wore out at least three such storybooks during our children's early years. The children often sat on the floor listening to their mother tell them stories while she was ironing or washing dishes.

Children must also learn reverence for God, for His Word and for His house during the preschool years. Here, as always, you will be teaching more by example than by precept. A child will respond to the Bible in much the same way that he sees his parents respond to it.

Stories other than those based on the Bible can be profitably used to teach as well as to entertain your child. Many good stories are available that help teach honesty, kindness, obedience, helpfulness, respect, thrift and resourcefulness. At this early age these stories are also enjoyed over and over again and thus mold character. Missionary stories also help direct the child's thinking.

A child loves to help and wants to do what he sees his mother or father do. Let him help as much as possible. His willingness to work later on might hinge on your efforts and patience with him as he tries to help you in ordinary tasks as a small child. This requires patience and much grace. A Christian parent must depend on the Lord in such matters.

Scripture Memorization

The memorization of scripture should begin during the preschool age as soon as the child learns to talk. The best method may be to teach complete verses and begin with scriptures that pertain to salvation Romans 3:23; 6:23; John 1:12; Ephesians 2:8,9; Titus 3:5; John 3:16; 5:24; I John 5:12.

At this age a child memorizes basically by repetition, and for this reason he may learn only one verse in a month. Say a verse to him as he gets ready for bed. Repeat it over and over, and ask him to say it with you. Make it a game. Soon, he will be able to repeat it by himself, not even aware of having worked at it. Even the reference can be taught in this way to a small child. A child can easily learn 20 or more verses by the time he enters kindergarten.

You will find that as a child memorizes scripture, he will begin asking questions about the verses. This is another opportunity to enlighten him concerning divine truth. As soon as you notice the working of the Spirit in convicting your child of sin, watch for the right moment to bring him to a saving knowledge of the Lord Jesus. All of our children accepted Jesus Christ as their Saviour before they were six years of age.

Teaching is basically the imparting of knowledge. True teaching organizes that knowledge and makes it simple and easy to understand. Christian truth must be simplified, set in order, imparted, made to be understood and applied.

We cannot overemphasize the great importance of the parents' own personal devotional time. It is so necessary as a preparation for leading our children properly. Here is our simple formula for making time for proper devotional periods:

1. Jot down all the things that you do, regularly or irregularly. If possible, estimate how much time each one takes.

2. Classify and number them according to their importance, putting first things first. Be sure your classification is in accordance with God's desire for your life.

3. Adjust the time needed for the important duties.

4. Eliminate as many of the less important things as necessary to give you the proper time for your devotional period. Unless we plan this time we will never have time.

Children in Church

Training a child to be quiet in church often presents a real difficulty to parents. It is too easy to excuse his behavior on the basis that he is too young and doesn't know any better. The fact is that when a child is still very small, he can be taught reverence for God. We must teach him that the church building is the place where God's people worship Him together and where He talks to them through the minister and His Word.

As parents we must insist that our children be quiet when they enter the church. When we explain that we go there to meet God, this should not be so difficult, although it may take consistent and persistent training. Never let a child run or play in the church before, during or after the service. More irreverence for God's house is developed in children by their playing inside and outside the church, usually after the meetings, than in any other way.

Naturally, a small child will have to be kept busy during the church service; parents should always bring something along for this purpose. There are many little ways to keep the preschooler occupied so that he will not disturb anyone. He must be told again and again that any vigorous movements, such as standing up or running around, disturb other people and keep them from hearing what God has to say to them. Reverence for God must be instilled in the child.

However, if a child misbehaves, he should be punished. When he is small, the punishment should immediately follow the offense. It is sometimes necessary to take the child out of church for this. (Usually, parents with children sit toward the back of the church.) When the child is a little older and misbehaves, he should know that he will be punished as soon as he gets home. If this punishment is promised to him, it must be carried out, or he will conclude that your word means nothing.

Such training will take patience and will have to be repeated over and over again. Scolding at this point might actually defeat our purpose. Parents must remember Paul's admonition: "Ye fathers, provoke not your children to wrath" (Eph. 6:4). Another translation of this verse is: "Fathers, do not irritate and provoke your children to anger—do not exasperate them to resentment—but rear them [tenderly] in the training and discipline and the counsel and admonition of the Lord" (Amplified). Be sure to tell your child when he has been quiet that you really appreciated it and that God appreciated it. Praise can work wonders with children.

At Family Devotions

When the children are of preschool age, the family devotional time should be planned especially with them in mind. A parent can read or tell a Bible story, and a few short choruses may be sung. If there are school children in the home, it might be well to have a devotional period at the breakfast table for all the family. On the other hand, some parents may find it better to have a special period just for the younger ones soon after the other children have gone to school. All children seem to enjoy singing, and it is well worthwhile to teach the smaller ones some of the gospel hymns. Always keep in mind that the devotional period for the younger children should not be long.

Concerning prayer, explain to the child what you are doing and that God can hear our words. In fact, children need to be taught that God knows what we need without our telling Him but that He wants us to pray to Him anyway. Explain to the child what prayer really is.

A small child may be taught to pray just by asking him to tell the Lord "Thank You" for something that is dear to him. The parents can have the child repeat short sentences, stating some of the things for which we ask. After a few demonstrations like this the parents will be surprised at what the child will say. He may pray about some things which adults would consider silly but which are very important to him. We should never laugh at such prayers. If a little one persists in foolish praying, however, he should kindly be shown again how to pray. Have him repeat after you words that will teach him what true prayer is. In this way he will gradually learn to talk to God.

As the child begins to talk to God, he may soon begin to realize what sin really is and how holy God is. This realization will come if these matters are brought before him through the Word. Soon the parent may be able to lead him to accept the Lord Jesus Christ as his personal Saviour. Of course, this can only happen after there has been real conviction of sin.

You may find that bedtime is also a good time to teach your child about spiritual things. You may repeat a Scripture verse with him as he gets ready for bed. Then explain to him what the verse means. Kneel beside the bed with him, and pray with him and for him. If he has not yet learned to say his own prayer, ask him to say a prayer after you.

Children who have learned to read should join in reading at the devotional period. As soon as he can read, each child should have his own Bible with large enough print for easy reading.

In our home we followed the practice of having each one read a few verses. Father would begin, then Mother, then the children would read according to the way they were seated at the table.

Those in the early grades, who may stumble considerably with their reading, should read only one verse, or the older children may become discouraged. Parents should be helpful in pronouncing words for them. The older children can read three or four verses as soon as they have learned to read easily. This will help to keep their attention. If there are more children than can pray at one devotional period, the father should appoint one or two children to pray, making sure that all are eventually given the opportunity. Always one parent and at least one of the children should pray.

Family devotions is not the best time to teach children the words they should use in prayer. If a child needs help in learning to express himself, it should be given in private so he will not be embarrassed by the other children's presence. Do not encourage them to memorize a prayer, but urge them to think for themselves and be guided in their prayers by the Holy Spirit.

The Book of Proverbs gives much sound instruction concerning child training and discipline. Read it very often. And soon after the children reach school age, the Book of Proverbs can be read in the devotional period with the family at least once a year. Always keep in mind that our children should be aware of our love for them. This should be among their earliest recollections and basic memories as they grow older.

Children's Early School Years

When children begin school, they enter a very different era in their young lives. New and different problems face parents. They are often gripped by fear as little ones leave them and their protection and become subject to outside influences. But, as always, we must commit them to the Lord, trusting Him to keep them. He does the keeping even though He wants to do it through us.

If parental authority has been instilled during preschool years, the child will quite naturally submit to the authority of the teacher. There must be no letup, however, in teaching our growing children to respect authority and be subject to it. If difficulties arise between child and teacher, it is never wise to criticize the teacher even if the child feels he is not treated fairly. Problems should be discussed with the teacher in order to remove any difficulties and differences but not in the presence of the child. To instill respect and subjection to authority is of very great importance (Rom. 13:1-7).

Christian parents sometimes find that they cannot accept certain things that are taught to their children. Even here children can be guided in the right path if parents are careful to keep their confidence and to give reasons for their disagreement. For example, parents often ask whether their child should take part in such activities as folk dancing. A general opinion seems to be that in the early grades this is really harmless, and many parents think that we do not need to say anything about it. Our conviction is that attitudes toward such things as dancing are formed very early in life. If we allow dancing in the early grades, how can we expect the child to see a reason for not allowing it later on? We need to be consistent.

Usually, teachers are very gracious in excusing a child when the parents' position is explained. Kindly ask that some other responsibility be given to the child while the dancing class is in session. Such a situation can become a challenge to the child rather than a trial. It will be good for our children to learn at an early age that living for the Lord Jesus costs something.

At school, children hear things that they have never before been exposed to. They may come home using words and expressions that startle their parents. Often a child is entirely ignorant of the meaning of what he has said. However, it is the parents' duty to explain such words and not allow them to be repeated. Mother and Father must evidence not only patience, genuine love and kindness but also firmness. Teaching is a process and is done precept upon precept, line upon line, here a little and there a little, according to Isaiah 28:10. Again, consistency is of vital importance.

When a child begins his school life, new interests, new friends and the many hours of his day spent in school will make it necessary for his parents to carefully plan for his spiritual development. The family devotional time must not be neglected but strengthened. If the best time in your home for family devotions is in the evening, perhaps a few extra minutes should be spent in prayer in the morning just before the child leaves for school. Commit him to the Lord and ask Him to guide and direct him, as well as keep him, throughout the day. If a child is conscious of his parents' total dependence on the Lord for his well-being he, too, will begin to put his confidence and trust in the Lord.

In these days when the public schools are often filled with secular, humanistic philosophy and sinful activities, Christian parents should consider the pros and cons of sending their children to a Christian school, if one is available.

Systematic memorization of scripture should definitely be pursued. Children are forming habits; let one habit be the memorizing of God's Word. Review is an important part of memorizing, and this can become a game. The giving of awards might be very effective.

As the adventuresome little learner is encouraged to read, he should be shown the joy of finding out for himself what God says to him in His Word. There is real joy in seeing children reading God's Word at an early age. One of the first books a child should have is his own Bible, inexpensively bound but with clear, readable print. A "red letter" Bible is not the best, since it can easily give him a wrong view of the inspiration of the Scriptures.

The early school years are also great years for singing as a family. Happy hours can be spent in learning and singing hymns and gospel songs. Mrs. Epp says, "Some of the happiest memories of my childhood are the times when my sisters and I learned hymns and then sang them from memory while washing dishes. Normal children, either boys or girls, seem to have no natural love for washing dishes. But using that time to sing can even make dishwashing a delight. Since this was such a blessing to me in my childhood, we did this when our children were growing up. So this practice has become a blessing the second time in my life."

The Home

"Home" is a delightful word. For many of us it carries pleasant memories of many happy events. Home also suggests a place where one can relax and be oneself, a place where one is always wanted and loved. As Christian parents we have the privilege of establishing and maintaining a home, not just an address or a house in which to sleep and eat. We should try to make it a place of seclusion, love and companionship.

Many little things make up the home. While, as the Scriptures say, we are to always rejoice (Phil. 4:4), it is also true that our happiness depends primarily on little things that happen. Home can be a place of happiness because of the things that take place there.

To begin with, it is wise to teach a child from his infancy that he belongs at home. It is imperative that we instill in his heart a desire to stay at home. This must be done not only by what we say but also by our love and companionship. If he wants to leave the house or the yard, he must ask the permission of his parents. Parents should always know where their children are. But it is just as important that each child know where his parents are. A child should never be left to take care of himself.

In our home we had the rule that no child left our yard without permission. This sometimes seemed to be a hardship, especially to the children, but we always knew where they were. Then, in giving permission, we generally agreed on a time when they should be home again. This prevented many anxious moments, and the children knew exactly what was expected of them. Some may feel that we were overly cautious and that the children might have resented that rule. But this was not the case. When children are taught to obey such rules from the time they are small, they will feel more secure because they know exactly what is expected of them.

If you have a rule, you will also need a penalty for breaking the rule. This is where the parents need persistence and much patience. A rule that can be broken easily with no unhappy consequences is no rule at all.

In our home we made it clear to the children that if they left the yard without our permission, they would have to stay in the house for 24 hours. They could not go out to play with their friends during that time. To the little toddler who does not quite understand all the reasons for the rules, one can be a bit more lenient with the punishment; yet a child must be taught even before he really grasps the reasons that he is not to leave the yard. As soon as a child reaches a certain point in his growth, he can watch over the younger ones, reminding them that if they leave the yard they will have to stay in the house. Rules must be applied in love and kindness.

An example may help to illustrate this point. One of our children, when he was about eight or ten years of age, left the yard without permission. The penalty was immediately applied. Since this took place in the evening, he would have to stay indoors throughout the next day. The next morning, however, we found that during the night a cloudburst had sent a creek, which was normally 50 feet wide, out of its banks so that it was half a mile to a mile wide, and this was in town. Everybody, of course, wanted to go and see it.

We faced the question, Should we break the rule, or should we stick by it? This was a hard decision to make, because the flood was a once-in-a-lifetime sight which the child would naturally not want to miss. We talked it over with him, giving him the choice of either staying home and finishing out the 24 hours in the house while we went to see the flood or going with us to see the flood. If he chose the latter, he understood that the amount of time needed to see the flood was to be added to the penalty to make up the 24 hours. The child chose the latter. This agreement was strictly kept, and to our recollection we never again had to punish him for leaving the yard. He not only remembered the punishment, but he also remembered our love and kindness in not being unreasonable at such a time.

Home is for the children, so there should be room for them and their friends to play. Our backyard was a place where children grew and played at the expense of a lawn. To raise men and women who live forever is much more important than to have a lovely backyard for a few short years. It may be work and trouble to have the children of the neighborhood in your backyard, but you will know what your children are doing. Then, too, if they are at home, you can direct and control their activities.

Home should always be a place where the children have the privilege of bringing their playmates. They should want to bring their friends to their house. The mother should be willing to treat the children with cookies, if convenient—anything to make them feel they are wanted. In this way the playmates can be observed. If they are teaching our children wrong things, we can help our children by pointing out to them that they must be examples as Christians to a neighborhood which may not know Christ. We can show them that Christians do not do certain things. It is not enough to merely scold them for playing with unruly neighbors; we must show our children what is wrong conduct and what is right.

On one occasion some neighborhood children were playing in our yard. Their parents had the philosophy that children were never to be corrected. They were to be allowed to make their own decisions and do as they pleased. Their little boy broke off one or two of our small poplar trees which we had planted just the year before—he thought it was fun. His older brother was with him and told us politely that we were not to reprove the little fellow for what he had done.

This became quite a lesson to our children. If this had been my child, I would have taken the part of the tree that had been broken off and applied it in the proper manner, as the Bible teaches. But we were able to point out to our children what would happen to them if they ever did what their visitor had done. It became a good object lesson to them.

Family Chores

Children need to do some work in the home. To make a home, all of its members are needed. Even small children should be given small responsibilities. Little children love to help in the kitchen and can be taught to help even though it slows the mother's work down. Remember, we as parents are molding lives, and no amount of inconvenience is too great in achieving this goal. Here is where one can begin to teach them to do worthwhile things which will really help their parents.

The school-age children's chores around the house should be more numerous. Many unexpected tasks come up from day to day, but definite jobs should also be assigned to each individual. Perhaps a few things need to be done every day and others only on certain days. On the farm this is a little easier to accomplish, because farm chores are more numerous. Nevertheless, cleaning their rooms, taking care of their clothing, washing the dishes, vacuuming the rugs and many other tasks should be regular responsibilities for growing children.

When they bring schoolwork home to be done in the evenings, parents may have to help them. This does not mean doing the work for them. As parents take an interest in their children's studies, they become acquainted with what the children are being taught. Although it is not wise to criticize a

94

teacher or the school in the child's presence, the parents can learn what influences they may need to counteract.

As Christian parents we must keep in mind that Christian training is our responsibility. We may not always be able to help in the subject matter being studied by our children, but even a sympathetic parent is a real help. Sometimes a child needs to let his "safety valve" blow off. It is well to listen sympathetically and then encourage the child and not allow an attitude to prevail that will foster bitterness in the child against the teacher or the subject being studied.

Home is not only a place to learn to work and to teach Christian principles but also a place for parents and children to play together. Parents should set aside time for this. The kind of play differs with age, of course, but play is important. Many Christian principles can be learned while playing. Our children love to think back to the hours that we spent together playing checkers and dominoes and other types of games which encouraged their intellect. By playing these games with them, we taught them to be good losers as well as good winners.

In checkers we always tried to make it just as hard for them as we could. But we also encouraged them and gave them a pat on the back for their efforts if they beat their dad or mom. It is good to try to stay far enough ahead of them so that most of the time they have to exert themselves to be on the winning side. Then, too, it is good for them to express a little childish delight when they have been able to beat one of their parents. Again, this is a good time to teach them what false pride will do.

The Sunday Problem

Some Sunday problems can be solved by planning the proper use of Sunday afternoons. Sunday is, of course, the Lord's day. We never encouraged our children to leave their homework for Sunday but rather to give the Lord His time first.

Sunday afternoon in our home was a sort of family time, especially when the children were smaller. We often played checkers or bird games with them and kept our children home with us when it was practical. Sometimes they invited their friends to visit and they, too, joined in the games. We often gathered around the piano and had a family sing. The family still likes to do this when they are home.

I do not believe it is good for the Christian's children to be in the neighbor's yard playing games with the unsaved on Sunday or possibly running up and down alleys or going to questionable places. So this is one good way to keep them home and happy. If this is done while they are young, they will want to invite their friends over when they are older. Cookies, ice cream or some other treat should be on hand.

The schedule of church meetings must be kept in mind in planning Sunday activities, and young children may need time for naps.

Sometimes several of our children would be gone to visit friends on Sunday, and only one would be left at home. Mrs. Epp often spent most of the afternoon reading something special to whoever was left at home.

If a good home and family atmosphere is created and kept from the time the children are young, home becomes a place where they want to be. This love for home stays with them even when they are older and questionable things are more likely to compete for their attention. We must encourage the children to want to be at home. This calls for much understanding and planning.

In our first pastorate we tried to plan Sunday afternoon activities for the young people in the church. Teenagers love to sing, so we would take them to the jail for services once a month. We also frequently held services in a children's home in a neighboring town. Senior citizens' homes were also visited. In this manner our young people could see God working directly. They learned how to tell others about Christ, saw souls saved and began to experience a burden and passion for souls.

Today most of those young people are leaders in their churches. Some are missionaries, and the majority of the others are active in some sort of Christian work.

Always remember that we must do more than just tell children what is right and good—they must be led. This takes time, whether at home or in the church. Our children belong to God. He has given them to us for proper training that they might be prepared for His use.

The real compensation for us came some time ago. Our whole family (then 20 persons, including 4 in-laws and 9 grandchildren) was home for a final reunion before several of them left for mission work overseas. The highlight of the evening came when the children asked if we could have one of our family "sings." Mr. Epp thought it would be wonderful to sit back and listen, but he was not allowed to stay in his chair. "We need your bass voice, Dad," they insisted, so he joined them. Immediately our son-in-law, who was soon to leave for the mission field, ran for the tape recorder to record the whole session, not just the singing. He said, "We want this so that when we get lonely, we can have a little family visit again."

Our hearts are grateful to God for calling our children to the ministry of His Word.

Inducements to Bible Reading

A systematic method of Bible reading is a spiritually healthy thing for children as well as adults. But a definite program has to be outlined, and encouragement is needed along the way. Children can be induced to read their Bible regularly, either on the basis of a game or by compulsion. Too often, however, compulsion builds up resentment so that the Bible reading is of little benefit.

We pondered this matter for a long time and prayed about it a lot. We believe the Lord gave us a method which, for us, paid great dividends.

Before our oldest children reached high school, we agreed with them that when they had read their Bibles through four times on a systematic basis, we would reward them with a good, 17-jewel watch. This is something that virtually all children highly prize. But to read the Bible four times before they received any tangible reward was asking quite a bit of them. For this reason we designed other rewards to be given each time they read the Bible through. We varied these with each child. The final and best reward, of course, was presented when they had read the Bible through the fourth time, and this reward was the same for each one.

When one of our girls was about 11 years old, her interest in Bible reading began to lag. As an inducement I agreed to take her with me to a special summer youth conference where I was to be one of the principal speakers, provided she had read her Bible through by the end of June. As a further incentive I promised that if she finished her reading by the end of May, we would travel one way to the conference by airplane and the other by train, a total distance of about 750 miles. She responded so well that we were able to travel in that way. Years have passed since then, but she still greatly cherishes that experience.

Four of our children earned their watches, one by the age of 15, one at 17 and the third at 19. The fourth, the youngest one, determined that she was going to break all records and earn her watch before her 15th birthday. She earned it in her 14th year.

The systematic reading of the Bible has to be worked out for most of us. A free Bible reading schedule in pamphlet form can be obtained by writing to Back to the Bible and asking for number 4270-5. You can use it as a book marker in your Bible.

If the child wishes to complete a reading of the Bible in more or less time than a year, a schedule can be worked out to fit the need. For example, we used the Bible being read by our youngest daughter and divided the number of New Testament pages by the number of days needed to read it through. We did the same with the Old Testament. From this information we made a chart to help her keep track of her daily reading in both Testaments.

Some pleasant and humorous incidents related to the children's Bible reading stand out in our memories. When our older children were in junior high and high school, we also had a couple of missionary children in our home. This meant that there were five or six young people active in regular Bible reading. It often provided an interesting topic of discussion at the breakfast table. Our one son competed with his sisters and the two missionary girls, trying to keep ahead of them.

One particular incident that we often laugh about occurred one evening when my son and I were out together for the entire evening, returning around ten o'clock. He lost little time in getting to bed, but instead of going to sleep, he turned on his light and read his Bible chapters for the day. The older girls had missed him all evening, but they did not know he was with me. However, shortly after ten o'clock they noticed he was reading his Bible and concluded that he had spent the whole evening reading and had succeeded in getting way ahead of them. They decided there was only one thing for them to do. They sat up until after midnight catching up on their Bible reading so that he would not be ahead of them. We often laugh about this, but it was one misunderstanding that paid off.

The greatest benefits from Bible reading came in the good attitudes created in the children. Whenever they became quarrelsome or were upset with their teachers, their studies or things at home, usually a talk with them revealed that they had neglected their daily Bible reading. We encouraged them to get back on schedule immediately, and very soon we would see their attitudes change.

Some will ask the question, "Is this type of Bible reading which is based on awards and contests really going to accomplish anything?" My question is "Which is better, having them read their Bible or not read their Bible?" Paul once told the Philippians that some were preaching Christ out of contention and others out of good will. His joy was in the fact that Christ was being preached, whether out of contention or out of good will (see Phil. 1:15-18).

Our conclusion is that this type of Bible reading may not be all that one could wish for, but it is 99 percent better than no Bible reading. We have felt it become the stabilizing factor in our children's Christian walk. It was a helpful factor when they went to Bible school. They had a knowledge of the Bible not possessed by those who had not practiced some type of regular Bible reading.

Do something to induce your children to read their Bible. Devise your own method of encouragement—ours is just one method. Do not force this reading. After your children are in the second, third or fourth grades, they can begin a regular schedule of reading on a small scale. A good Bible reading program will pay dividends.

Training in Use of Money

Training children how to handle money is of great importance.

Many youngsters feel that they should have access to money from the time they enter grade school. This can serve a good purpose if we teach them how to handle it properly.

We found it acceptable to give our children a monthly allowance after their second or third year in school. The first allowance may be one or two dollars a month, which is not much, but it is a beginning.

We got each of the children a little account book and instructed them in a very simple form of bookkeeping. In one column they were to write the amount they received and in the second column the amount they spent. They were to list every item. At first we carefully checked the books with them once a month. We compared what they had marked down as having been spent with the amount they had received and the amount that was left. We tried not to be harsh with them if they did not get the books to balance, but our aim was to impress them with the need to write things down at the time the money was spent.

From the beginning we taught them that a portion of their allowance belonged to the Lord and that His portion must be set aside first. We let them choose how much they wanted to put into the Lord's portion. The church we attended followed the Faith Promise method of giving for missionary work. So we encouraged the children to promise God that they would give a certain portion through this method once a month. Out of a two-dollar allowance they would give as much as 50 cents to missions.

As they grew older, usually about the time they entered junior high school, we increased the allowances. Then when they became ninth graders, and later when they became seniors in high school, we increased it again.

As we went over the books with them each month, we could quietly point out to them money that was spent foolishly, but usually we said very little. The very fact that they had to give an account was usually enough to make them conscious of spending their money wisely.

If they were careless, the money would be spent before the month was over. Then they would have to go without. So they soon learned to make it stretch. They would also save some for Christmas or for special gifts. Sometimes several months before Christmas they would consult with us about jobs they could do to earn extra money. We tried to arrange this for them. We did not pay them to do their regular chores but gave them extra tasks that normally would not be their responsibility.

When they were older, we did not always make a monthly check of their books. We let them know that we had full confidence in them. When they entered junior high school, we taught them a more detailed, three-column bookkeeping system with columns for money received, money paid out and the balance left. By keeping a second page on the Lord's funds, we taught them how to transfer from the regular fund to the Lord's fund. All of this taught them to be thrifty—acquainted with money and yet learning to save it. We never gave them so much that they in any way felt free to spend it on luxuries.

Some families arrange for their children to get jobs—a paper route, lawn mowing, snow shoveling, babysitting and so on. From these earnings they are often expected to buy for themselves certain items of clothing. We have done very little of this, but it is a method that many have used to good advantage.

One other approach was very helpful. Sometimes the children would want something that we as parents thought was unnecessary. We would not buy it for them, but if they insisted month after month, and if we felt that it was not a harmful thing, we would suggest, "All right, if you want that, you buy it." This had an immediate effect. They would ask themselves, "Do I really want it badly enough to use my allowance or my extra earnings for it?" Many times they decided they did not want it after all. At other times they did, and they were satisfied that they had bought it with their own money.

Conclusion

We must always remember that God has given us our children, not for ourselves or our pleasure but for Himself. He has given them to us so that we might be the instruments in His hands to properly train them for His purposes. We must always remember that it is not enough to point them to Christ. This is imperative, of course, and must be done early. But then we need to instill in their hearts the purpose for which we are on earth. Our overall purpose is to be ambassadors of the Lord Jesus Christ. This does not mean that everyone is going to be a missionary or a preacher, but every believer is an appointed ambassador. None of us can resign from this responsibility; it is a God-appointed duty (II Cor. 5:18-20). Consequently, we must prepare so that we can fit into whatever ministry God has for us.

With this in mind, we never thought of considering anything but Bible school training for our children. This was necessary, basic training. There never was a question in the hearts and minds of our children, as far as we know, but that Bible school was the next step in their education after high school.

In our experience this has paid large dividends. Whether the children go into full-time Christian service or not, it gives them a basis for whatever ministry God may have for them. Those who have gone on to college have stated that their Bible school training gave them a foundation on which to stand, even though they attended a Christian college.

Parents will be held responsible for the training of their children for the ministry to which God has appointed them. We are not to train them merely for ourselves or even to think of keeping them merely for ourselves. They are given to us for a while to be given back to Him permanently. Keep this in mind, even as you begin to teach your preschool-age child the basic principles of a God-given plan for his or her life.

Family Devotions

by Robert S. Peterson

This chapter was prepared especially to provide help often asked for by Christians with young and growing families. Rev. Robert S. Peterson is administrative director of Editorial and Counseling at the Back to the Bible Broadcast. He writes from many years of experience gained as a pastor, as a counselor and as a Christian parent.

Family Devotions

Family devotions are important, for the family that worships together is more likely to stay together. Many of us never seem to have enough time to do the things we ought to do, so we must deliberately set aside time to do the most important things each day. Devotions are so important to the spiritual health of those in the home that Satan will do his best to keep the family from meeting together to read the Bible and pray. But we must not allow anyone or anything to rob us of this important time together. In Psalm 27:8 we read: "When thou saidst, Seek ye my face; my heart said unto thee, Thy face, Lord, will I seek." The children learn to worship the Lord and to pray for one another in family devotions.

It is difficult for small children to sit still for very long; however, they can and must be taught to be quiet and to respond when they are given an opportunity to take part. The devotional period should be simple, understandable and short if the children are small. Even a very young child can learn to be reverent during devotions. It is not hard to teach him to bow his head in reverence to God and to close his eyes, shutting out anything that would distract.

The Time

Morning is often the best time for the family to meet together. If the father leaves for work very early, however, it would be better to meet in the evening, perhaps at the supper hour. If possible the entire family should participate on a regular basis. In a large family each child may take part only once or twice a week, but each one should know that he has an important part.

Scripture

The Scripture portion to be read should be chosen in advance so there is no searching for a passage after the family has gathered. Remember, it is not how much we read but how carefully the Scriptures are applied that brings spiritual help and refreshment. We ought to emphasize one truth each day. Perhaps for the sake of variety we should ask questions about the story or about the Scripture portion read. This will stimulate interest and encourage the children to listen carefully. A devotional guide that is written for children and young people will prove helpful. Write to Back to the Bible for a free Literature Catalog (number 4255-1), which describes a number of aids for family devotions and for your personal quiet time.

Scripture Memory

Scripture memory should be included in family devotions. Children find it easy to memorize scripture, and scripture stored in the heart will bring eternal dividends. "Thy word have I hid in mine heart, that I might not sin against thee" (Ps. 119:11). Be sure to commend the children for memorizing God's Word, and remind them to review the Scripture portions from the previous week.

Prayer

Before praying, give the members of the family an opportunity to voice their prayer requests and to tell of answers to prayer. As we stop and consider what God has done for us in the past, we are encouraged to trust Him for even greater things in the future. "Be careful for nothing; but in every thing by prayer and supplication with thanksgiving let your requests be made known unto God. And the peace of God, which passeth all understanding, shall keep your hearts and minds through Christ Jesus" (Phil. 4:6,7). Be sure to teach the children to make their requests known with thanksgiving.

We teach our children to pray by praying in their presence. The children must hear us pray for them and their daily needs. This assures them of our love for them and encourages them to pray for each other. It is very important that each child be taught to pray in his or her early years. While a memorized prayer will provide a starting point for preschool children, they should soon learn to express their own requests in their own words.

There may be times when one of the children has a personal problem that should not be mentioned in family devotions. This can be prayed for in private.

Guard against using the devotional period for discipline. If Johnny did something wrong while his father was at work, this should be dealt with, but not at the table or at family devotions.

Soon after the Apostle Peter denied the Lord, the Saviour provided a meal for the 11 disciples. Peter, of course, was included. The Lord said graciously, "Come and dine. And none of the disciples durst ask him, Who art thou? knowing that it was the Lord. Jesus then cometh, and taketh bread, and giveth them, and fish likewise" (John 21:12,13). This meal was eaten without reference to Peter's denial. The dinner table is not the place to have a court trial. Not until after they had eaten this meal did the Lord Jesus graciously deal with Peter (vv. 15-17).

Family devotions should maintain a refreshing atmosphere. Children who have been raised in this atmosphere will establish a family altar when they grow up and have a family of their own.

As Christian parents faithfully maintain their family devotional times, we are confident that their children will one day rise up and call them "blessed" (Prov. 31:28).

110

Makε a good marriagε or Makε a good marriagε better

Stop, Love and Listen
J. Allan Petersen. Ask not what your marriage can do
for you. Find out what you can do for your marriage.
$1.00 each   1125-7

Happy Family Life
Henry Brandt and Homer Dowdy. Husband and wife
teamwork and how to make it work.
50¢ each   1146-X